POLITICAL PARTIES AND CIVIL SOCIETY
IN FEDERAL COUNTRIES

A Global Dialogue on Federalism publications available
BOOK SERIES
*Constitutional Origins, Structure, and Change in Federal Countries* (2005), Volume 1
*Distribution of Powers and Responsibilities in Federal Countries* (2006), Volume 2
*Legislative, Executive, and Judicial Governance in Federal Countries* (2006), Volume 3
*The Practice of Fiscal Federalism: Comparative Perspectives* (2007), Volume 4
*Foreign Relations in Federal Countries* (2009), Volume 5
*Local Government and Metropolitan Regions in Federal Systems* (2009), Volume 6
*Diversity and Unity in Federal Countries* (2010), Volume 7
BOOKLET SERIES
*Dialogues on Constitutional Origins, Structure, and Change in Federal Countries* (2005), Volume 1
*Dialogues on Distribution of Powers and Responsibilities in Federal Countries* (2005), Volume 2
*Dialogues on Legislative, Executive, and Judicial Governance in Federal Countries* (2006), Volume 3
*Dialogues on the Practice of Fiscal Federalism: Comparative Perspectives* (2006), Volume 4
*Dialogues on Foreign Relations in Federal Countries* (2007), Volume 5
*Dialogues on Local Government and Metropolitan Regions in Federal Countries* (2007), Volume 6
*Dialogues on Diversity and Unity in Federal Countries* (2008), Volume 7
*Dialogues on Intergovernmental Relations in Federal Systems* (2010), Volume 8

Select Global Dialogue publications are available in other languages including
Arabic, French, German, Portuguese and Spanish. For more information on
what is available, visit www.forumfed.org.

A Global Dialogue on Federalism
Booklet Series
*Volume 9*

# POLITICAL PARTIES AND CIVIL SOCIETY
# IN FEDERAL COUNTRIES

EDITED BY RUPAK CHATTOPADHYAY
AND KARL NERENBERG

*Published by*

 **Forum of Federations**

*and*

## iacfs
INTERNATIONAL ASSOCIATION OF
CENTERS FOR FEDERAL STUDIES

*Marketed by*

McGill-Queen's University Press
Montreal & Kingston • London • Ithaca

© Forum of Federations, 2011
ISBN: 9780773537408

This publication was produced with generous financial support from the
Swiss Agency for Development and Cooperation and the Government of Canada.

---

Library and Archives Canada Cataloguing in Publication

Dialogues on political parties and civil society in federal countries / edited by
Rupak Chattopadhyay and Karl Nerenberg.

(A global dialogue on federalism booklet series ; v. 9)
ISBN 978-0-7735-3740-8

     1. Political parties. 2. Civil society. 3. Federal government.
I. Chattopadhyay, Rupak II. Nerenberg, Karl III. International Association
of Centers for Federal Studies IV. Forum of Federations
V. Series: Global dialogue on federalism booklet series ; v. 9


JF2051.D53 2010     324.2'04     C2010-905612-4

---

Printed and bound in Canada by Imprimerie Gauvin

MIX
Paper from
responsible sources
FSC® C100212

# Contents

# Preface

We are pleased to introduce this booklet on *Political Parties and Civil Society*, volume nine in the Global Dialogue Booklet series. This booklet offers a comparative overview of the subject across twelve federal systems, including: Australia, Belgium, Canada, Germany, India, Malaysia, Mexico, Nigeria, South Africa, Spain, Switzerland and the United States. Each of these countries has something unique to bring to this important examination of a vital and basic element of democracy.

Over-all, what a reader might conclude from this Booklet is that the political party system of each federal country appears to have developed in its own distinct way, and indeed this in turn has had an impact in the federalization of these countries. The fact of a multi-level, federal system has significant implications for political parties, but there are also many other crucial historic and cultural factors.

And so, at one end of the spectrum we have the Belgian system, where all parties are, in essence, linguistic and regional; while, at the other end, there is the American system where, its two party system consisting of the Democrats and Republicans at levels of government. Between the two, there are countries such as Canada and India, where there is a mixture of national and regional/provincial parties at the sub-national and federal levels of government.

The Canadian case is interesting, and illustrative of how difficult it can often be for outsiders to penetrate the subtle, complex — and not always rational or logical — folkways of a country's party system.

In 1998, the erstwhile leader of Canada's federal Progressive Conservative Party took over the leadership of the Liberal Party of Quebec (ultimately getting elected Premier of that province). At the time, many foreign observers asked why the onetime Conservative had chosen to switch parties. The answer was that he had not, necessarily, given up being a *federal* Conservative. The Liberal Party of *Quebec* is a distinct entity from the Liberal Party of *Canada*, and one can be, simultaneously, a provincial Liberal and federal Conservative — as, indeed, many are. In Canada, this is not true of all parties, or all provinces, and you almost have to be part of the local political culture to appreciate those distinctions.

The articles in the volume give the reader a privileged, "insider's perspective" on this sort of complex phenomenon. The articles will enable you to understand the American, German, Indian or South African party systems in much the same way as well-informed citizens of those countries do. In India, for example, the proliferation of regional parties and the advent of coalition governments at the national level have contributed to the federalization of the political system. This has simultaneously led to the emergence, as Sandeep Shastri notes, of a dualist structure when it comes to competitive party politics — with multi-party competition at the federal level and bi-partisan competition within the states.

Political parties are as crucial to healthy democracies as constitutions, yet they do not always receive the respect they are due. We too often think of constitutional democracy as noble and enlightened, while "politics" can be crass and very down-to-earth. This booklet affirms the central and vital role of political parties in the practice of democratic federalism.

What follows is as much a descriptive as a theoretical exercise. The authors provide a guided tour over the rough and irregular terrain of their countries' civil society and political party systems — and it is a fascinating tour, at that. The authors' observations are acute and insightful, and often unsparing. They show you their own countries' "rough terrain" as it is — hills, valleys, swamps, rocky crags and all!

That is why booklets such as this one, and the series of which it is a part, can be of such value. They can provide practitioners and researchers alike with a window into the real-life challenges of federalism in vastly different political, cultural and economic circumstances. We hope that, in so doing, we help improve both the practice and the understanding of federalism as a world-wide phenomenon.

In due course this booklet will be followed by a more comprehensive book on the same topic, wherein the authors of the booklet explore the theme in further detail. Both publications, which are part of the Global Dialogue on Federalism Series, are the outcome of a greater project led by two partner organizations, the Forum of Federations and the International Association of Centers for Federal Studies.

The Global Dialogue program explores federal governance by theme and aims to bring experts together to inspire new ideas and fill a gap in the comparative literature on federal governance. After presenting the ninth booklet in seven years, we note that these handy publications are becoming an indispensable reference document on their own, delivering instant comparative information on various topics in a concise format. It is not surprising that the previous volumes proved to be very popular and have been translated into numerous languages, including Arabic and Kurdish.

In this Booklet, the various aspects of political parties and civil society are described in country chapters entitled "Dialogue Insights". The chapters are introduced by a text of comparative reflections written by Klaus Detterbeck and Wolfgang Renzsch the theme coordinators. A glossary at the end of the booklet enhances the knowledge-sharing and educational vocation of this publication.

The questions the authors address include:

☐ How important are political parties and civil society organizations for the actual working of the federal system?

☐ In which ways do parties and civil society organizations have an impact and, specifically, what is their political role in federalism (e.g., as forces of national integration and/or regional pressure, as informal channels of intergovernmental bargaining, or as mediators or agents of territorial conflict)?

☐ What can we say about the dynamics of change? Do changes in party politics and civil society affect the guiding ideas, institutions and public policies of a federal system, even if there are no constitutional changes?

☐ What is the relation between parties and civil society?

☐ Is there a clear separation between the two types of political organization or are there elements that are interlocking?

☐ Is there competition between parties and civil society in the pursuit of political influence?

☐ Are territorial conflicts and the future of the federation an important source of political conflict?

☐ How important are regionalist and ethno-nationalist parties and civil society organizations? In what ways are such cleavages accommodated within the federal system?

These are only a small number of the questions that this series of articles addresses. As do some federal systems, this Booklet takes an *asymmetric* approach to its subject. The articles do not all answer the same questions, in an identical way. True to their own circumstances and cultures, the authors have examined the subject in a variety of ways, which underscores the diversity and complexity of federalism as it is practiced.

What makes the Global Dialogue booklet and book series nearly unique is the process by which the publications are generated.

Each theme process entails multiple stages, starting with the selection of a "theme coordinator". It is this person's task to create an internationally comprehensive set of questions covering institutional provisions and how they work in practice, based on the most current research. These sets of questions are the foundation of the program, as they guide the dialogue at the roundtables and ensure consistency in the book chapters. The roundtables themselves are led by a "country coordinator", and are organized concurrently in twelve chosen countries.

To create the most accurate picture of the situation in each country, the country coordinators invite a group of practicing and academic experts with diverse viewpoints and experience who are prepared to share with and learn from others in a non-politicized environment. At the end of the day, the coordinators are equipped to write an article that reflects the highlights of the dialogue from each country roundtable. The articles presented here have been generated from such an exchange.

Once each country has held its roundtable, representatives gather at an international roundtable to identify commonalities and differences and to generate new insights. Such insights are incorporated into the country chapters in the aforementioned theme book. The chapters reflect the fact that their authors were able to explore the theme from a global vantage point, resulting in a truly comparative exploration of the topic.

The success of the Global Dialogue Program depends fully on the engagement of a variety of organizations and dedicated individuals. For their generous financial support we would like to thank the Government of Canada and the Swiss Agency for Development and Cooperation. The International Roundtable in Berlin, Germany was made possible with generous support from the Academy of the Konrad Adenauer Foundation. We also wish in particular to acknowledge the experts who took part in the dialogue events for providing a diversity of perspectives that helped to shape the articles themselves. Klaus Detterbeck and Wolfgang Renzsch the Theme Coordinators, John Kincaid, Senior Editor of the book series, and the rest of the Global Dialogue Editorial Board have offered their invaluable advice and expertise. Thank you to Alan Fenna for doing the painstaking work of creating the glossary. We would like to acknowledge the support offered by several staff members at the Forum of Federations: Rhonda Dumas, Phillip Gonzalez, Roderick Macdonell, Chris Randall, and Carl Stieren. We would like to thank the staff at Imprimerie Gauvin for their important assistance in the printing process. Finally, we thank the staff at McGill-Queen's University Press for offering their support and advice throughout the publication process.

The Global Dialogue on Federalism Series continues the Forum of Federations' tradition of publishing either independently or in partnership with other organizations.

The Forum has produced a variety of books and multimedia material. For further information on the Forum's publications and activities, refer to the Forum's website at www.forumfed.org. The website contains links to other organizations and an on-line library which includes Global Dialogue articles and chapters.

The increasing body of literature produced by the Forum of Federations and the International Association of Centers for Federal Studies aims to encourage practitioners and scholars to use the knowledge gained to devise new solutions and to join the many active participants around the world in the growing international network on federalism. We welcome feedback and suggestions on how these series can be improved to serve this goal.

Rupak Chattopadhyay and Karl Nerenberg, Editors,
Forum of Federations

POLITICAL PARTIES AND CIVIL SOCIETY
IN FEDERAL COUNTRIES

# Comparative Reflections: Parties and Civil Society in Federal Systems

KLAUS DETTERBECK / WOLFGANG RENZSCH

Interest mediation between society and the political institutions of the state is one of the crucial elements of the democratic process. Political parties and civil society organizations can be seen as the most important intermediary groups in contemporary democracies. In focusing on federal democracies, the specific conditions of interest mediation in compound policies in which political sovereignty and competences are divided but also shared can be explored. While federalism shapes the ways parties compete and organize, parties as central actors in parliaments and governments have a decisive impact on federal dynamics. In a similar vein, the structures and behavioural norms of civil society, which are in part influenced by federal institutions, will come to co-determine federal dynamics.

Academic research has long neglected the significance of these mutual interactions. Party research has traditionally been dominated by sociological and historical approaches which had in common that parties were perceived as creations of civil society, or to be more precise, as expressions of the cleavages and fundamental conflicts of a given society. Despite some classical works in the field, the institutional aspects of parties did not receive much attention. If institutions were taken into account, electoral systems and the parliamentary or presidential mode of government figured more prominently than the territorial nature of the state.

Research on federalism, on the other hand, has often noticed the importance of political parties but has made relatively little use of this observation for analytical purposes. Studies focused on the constitutional design of the federation, the distribution of competences and fiscal resources or other important aspects of the federal design. However, the political actors who were driving the processes of federal decision-making were hardly seen as party representatives who are engaged in political competition and committed to specific programmatic goals.

In more recent years, the intellectual gap between party research and federalism studies has been narrowed. Bridges between the two academic communities have been built and more comprehensive frameworks have been developed.

The growing emphasis on the impact of civil society on politics has helped to overcome former boundaries in academic research. Theme Nine of the Global Dialogue series thus comes at the right time to give a fascinating insight into the complex patterns of mutual interaction between political parties, civil society and federal institutions in federations around the world.

## Themes of the Booklet

Looking across the country dialogues which will follow a number of themes can be identified for comparative reflections. First, several authors discuss the repercussions of one-party dominance on federal dynamics. In India, Malaysia, Mexico and South Africa a dominant party has been (or still is) at the centre of federal politics for an extended period of time. Starting out as liberation movements, these "catch-all parties" have brought together a variety of social forces and fostered the process of national integration. However, hegemonic party control over the whole territory has weakened the federal dispersal of powers. Civil society organizations were either incorporated via corporatist arrangements or remained relatively weak and distant to the dominant party regime.

Still, federalism has proved to be a powerful weapon for opposition parties to challenge one-party hegemony. Recent elections have brought remarkable changes to the structures of power in these countries, making pluralism and political competition more vibrant. This is probably most pronounced in India, while the ANC in South Africa remains in control in almost all provinces. The Nigerian case can be read as a counter-example. A highly centralized federal system leaves little space for a territorial separation of powers, so (multi-ethnic) parties compete for the "only show in town".

Second, the decline of traditional party allegiances is a recurrent theme in the country dialogues (e.g., Australia, Canada, Germany). Major parties which have dominated federal processes and organized agreements between the territorial levels have been losing hold (to some degree). The fragmentation of party systems is bringing in new political forces representing alternative sets of interests and identities. This is also coupled with public demands for more direct political participation. In general, there tend to be more players in the federal game nowadays.

Third, new sectors within civil society have become stronger in many countries (e.g., Belgium, Spain, Switzerland, India, Malaysia). Focusing on issues like citizens' rights, environmental protection or gender equality these groups tend to maintain a stronger distance to both political parties and state institutions compared to more established interest groups like trade unions and business associations. These new groups are more likely to be critical of old-style party politics and to act as rivals to parties in the articulation of social interests.

More generally speaking, the country dialogues show very different modes of relations between parties and civil society. At one end of the spectrum one could place the hegemony of party as seen in the cases of one-party dominance. At the other end of the spectrum, established interest groups which have a very strong position in the policy process and a strong voice inside the parties can be found in Switzerland. In between, there are cases in which strong linkages between individual parties and specific segments of civil society exist. Within the framework of a party democracy, the major interest groups are vital part of the process of devising and implementing public policies in countries like Australia, Belgium, Germany and Spain. Other cases, mainly Canada and the US, show a stronger separation between parties and civil society. In seeking pluralist access to government, a wide array of civil society organizations may work together with the major parties but maintain some distance. As already mentioned, new groups in civil society are generally less tied to any specific party.

Fourth, several country dialogues discuss processes of federal decentralization as important features of change. In some cases, strengthening the regional level has been seen as response to supranational integration and economic internationalization (e.g., Germany, Canada). In other cases, territorial conflict and the advocacy of ethno-nationalist parties have been driving forces (e.g., Belgium, Canada, Spain). Either way, party competition has often taken a regional turn. Politics at the sub-state level has become more autonomous. This has added to the stronger party system fragmentation at the central level and led to more diversity between regions.

Fifth, country dialogues have touched upon the question of a federal culture (e.g., Canada, USA). This has opened up debates, whether this refers to the willingness of both political actors and citizens to establish linkages between the territorial levels and to welcome federal cooperation and bargaining, or whether this is to accept federal autonomy and regional divergence. Finding the right balance between unity and diversity will remain an on-going task in all federal systems.

### The Role of Parties in Federal Systems

The country dialogues show quite clearly that the interaction between parties, civil society and federal institutions works differently in different places. The federal role of parties is subject to the political and social context of the federation. Party agency is another important aspect. The competitive strategies of political parties and their internal organization will have a strong impact on the integration of territorial levels.

While this calls for a case study approach of individual federations, the country dialogues still allow for detecting some more general patterns. In order to make sense of the diversity of phenomena, five different patterns can be identified. The main distinguishing feature is the specific way in which party politics has an impact on federal developments — the federal mechanics of party competition:

   □ a hegemonic model: federal systems in which a dominant party controls a rather centralized process of policy-making across the territorial levels. Regional interests may be articulated by factions within the dominant party representing specific federal units. South Africa can be seen as approaching this model best, whereas hegemony has become challenged in Malaysia and Mexico and has faded in India. The centralized Nigerian federation has given rise to a hegemonic position of the party holding the presidency;

☐ a cooperative model: federal systems in which vertically integrated parties organize a coordinated process of policy-making. Party negotiations, both internally and between parties in intergovernmental arenas, structure federal dynamics. While partisan veto players are important, strong cooperation between party governments at different levels may shift the balance towards federal centralization. Germany falls most clearly into this category, arguably Australia could be added;

☐ a competitive model: federal systems in which a holding-together centre is confronted with strong regional forces heading towards increased autonomy. Political negotiations inside the multi-level organizations and between parties are of crucial importance for federal dynamics. The latter may tend more strongly towards state decentralization. Among our country cases, Spain and (with some peculiarities) Belgium fulfil the criteria here;

☐ a decentralized model: federal systems in which regional autonomy is a vital aspect of both political parties and the federal design. The focus of parties is on the regional level with national organizations playing a coordinating role. Federal negotiations between territorial levels of government have a rather bureaucratic outlook and are less party-based. Switzerland and the USA come close to this model, Australia may also be placed in this category.

☐ a bifurcated model: federal systems in which the lack of vertical party integration accentuates the differences between territorial arenas. Parties stick to their specific constituencies which have a regional and/or linguistic basis. Intergovernmental relations between territorial levels may either be troubled by party conflict or removed from party politics via a more executive style of federalism. Canada (with different modes of integration among the major parties) and Belgium (without a single polity-wide party) resemble this model.

**Concluding Remarks**

Federal institutions, party competition and civil society are far from being static. There is permanent movement within all three spheres, making the interaction between them highly dynamic. The country dialogues aptly demonstrate the significant amount of changes that federal democracies have experienced in recent decades. Change has to do with the transformation of governance within nation-states. Yet, change has also been triggered by new forces within civil society and new dynamics of party competition. With the growing multiplicity and heterogeneity of political actors, the processes of interest mediation in federal systems have become more complex. Profound changes in the social and political bases of compound polities are providing new challenges for theorists and practitioners of federalism.

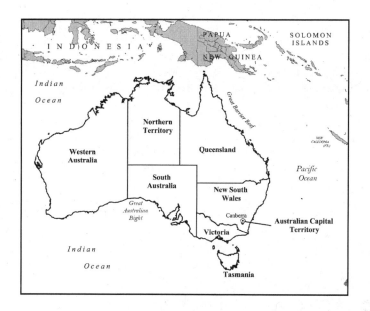

# Australia:
# The Decline of Party Allegiance

## NORMAN ABJORENSEN

For the best part of a century, Australia has operated under a classic two-party system (or, to some, a two-and-a-half party system, if one includes rural-based Nationals, formerly known as the Country Party). In line with that of many other western democracies, Australia is experiencing a declining allegiance to its major political parties, as the parties themselves decline in membership — phenomena that reflect long-term social change, with significant implications for civil society.

At the creation of the Australian federation in 1901, the new and rising Australian Labor Party, with its origins in the industrial labour movement, vied with liberal protectionists and conservative free traders for influence in the new parliament which, by the second election in 1903, had divided into three roughly equal groups. The instability and uncertainty brought about by shifting alliances drove the protectionists and free traders to bury their differences and unite against the Labor Party in 1909 in a so-called *Fusion*. The resulting two-party system has prevailed since then.

For much of the twentieth century, political struggles were essentially class-based, with industrial and agricultural workers supporting the Labor Party and urban professionals, the middle classes and land owners supporting the non-Labor parties which have gone under a variety of names. For 70 of those 100 years, the major non-Labor party governed in coalition with the smaller rural non-Labor party. The Labor Party, in government less often, suffered three damaging splits in that period: over conscription in the First World War, policy responses to the Great Depression in 1931-1932 and over the issue of communist influence in the trade unions in the 1950s.

Gradual changes in post-war society saw a rapid expansion of tertiary education, along with a decline in the agricultural workforce and a steady growth in the services sector as manufacturing — most of it sustained through high tariff protection — gradually became less significant as a major employment sector.

The Liberal Party, formed in 1944, strove to emulate Labor in forming a mass party with a permanent secretariat, and reached out to many workers in the lower middle class with a message based on greater prosperity and a fear of communism. Labor, for its part, also began to target the middle classes as the old class-based paradigm became blurred.

> The blurring of hitherto sharp class lines has had a significant impact on the way in which people tend to self-identify and on the parties themselves.

The blurring of hitherto sharp class lines has had a significant impact on the way in which people tend to self-identify and on the parties themselves. Up until 1970, close to 90 per cent of the electorate professed a strong allegiance to one or other of the major parties, and electoral contests were regularly targeted at the so-called "swing voters" who comprised the other 10 per cent. With compulsory voting in Australia since the 1920s, election campaigns too often resembled bidding wars to secure the uncommitted vote.

Data collected in the continuing Australian Political Attitudes and Australian Election Study surveys show a steady decline since 1970 in the number of people identifying with one or the other main parties — the percentage having fallen in 2004 to 77 per cent. The measured shift has been split between those who identify with a minor party and those who no longer identify with any party at all. Since the early 1990s, there has been a doubling of those identifying with minority parties, most notably the now defunct Australian Democrats and the rising Greens. Even more significant, however, has been the four-fold increase since 1970 of those who do not identify with any party at all. There are also perceived changes within these aggregate trends. For instance there is a noticeable decline in the strength of party identification.

While all parties, with the possible exception of the Greens, report a declining membership base, precise figures of party membership tend to be closely guarded. However, there are reports from each of the major parties in different states that have found their way into the public arena and that suggest a remarkably similar picture of both decline and disengagement.

In 2005, when the Labor Party opened the election of its national president to the party rank-and-file, 39,000 ballot papers were distributed but only 19,000 returned. This suggests a very small proportion of the Australian populations of about 21 million are party members, active or otherwise. A report in 2005 on the Labor Party in New South Wales, Australia's most populous state, revealed just 8000 members in that state who worked for a living (that is, excluding retired people) out of a total workforce of 3.25 million.

A continuing problem for Labor is its reliance on the union movement, itself in sharp decline, with coverage of less than 15 per cent of the private sector workforce. Given the unions' decisive influence in party counsels, Labor finds it increasingly difficult to break its traditional shackles to the union movement regardless of its declining adherence in the broader working community.

Similarly, in Victoria, Australia's second most populous state, where the conservative Liberal Party has traditionally been strong, an internal party review in 2008 showed that it had just 13,000 members, down from a peak of 46,000 in 1950 out of a much smaller population. More tellingly, the Liberal Party's median age stood at 62 against a median age of the population of 43. This suggests that citizen participation in political parties is neither extensive nor representative of the wider population.

There is also evidence of growing disenchantment with politics and politicians. While in many countries this can be reflected in a low voter turnout, Australia's compulsory voting sees it manifested in other ways, such as voters increasingly resorting to a split vote in supporting a major party for the House of Representatives but a minor party for the proportionally-elected upper house, the Senate.

This apparent decline in the social bases of both parties stands in contrast to the Greens, who now have members in most state parliaments as well as the Federal Senate. The Greens grew out of the environmental social movement of the 1980s and even today resemble a social movement more than they do a political party, with their rejection of hierarchical structures and commitment to member participation in policy development. A steadily increasing Green vote in inner urban electorates is now threatening a traditional Labor stronghold and this trend, if continued, suggests longer term realignment. It could also cause a "re-think" of how parties organize and relate to their bases.

# Political Parties and Civil Society in Belgium

LIEVEN DE WINTER /
CAROLINE VAN WYNESBERGHE

Political parties are the key actors in the emergence and transformation of Belgium's peculiar federal model, as well its federal/state coordination — and, perhaps, the eventual disintegration of the Belgian state. Belgium's main civil society organizations on the other hand, tend generally to play an accommodating role.

The Belgian federation is a very peculiar and eccentric one for several reasons.

First, its constituent unit structure is dual and consists of two types of partially overlapping entities. There are three cultural communities (the Flemish, French-speaking and German-speaking communities), and three regions (Flanders, Wallonia and Brussels).

A second element of asymmetry is that the Flemish region and community merged into a single unit with one regional government and parliament.

Third, there are now no federal parties in Belgium that encompass the entire country, but only French or Flemish parties, each representing its own community exclusively. They do not compete for votes across language lines, apart from in the large Brussels-Halle-Vilvoorde constituency. Hence, parties tend to contribute to centrifugal tendencies rather than act as agents of federal coordination and integration.

Fourth, regions and communities have been allotted large policy responsibilities. In cases of conflict between orders of government, there is no hierarchy between federal and constituent unit legislation. Finally, the Belgian federalization process has been the result of the separation of constituent units of a former unitary state. Many other federations were formed by bringing together previously distinct units.

These particular features are the product of a century long process of centre-periphery conflicts. While it took more than a century (since the foundation of Belgium as a French-speaking state in 1830) for the Flemish-speaking majority to obtain equal linguistic and cultural rights, after World War II the Flemish Movement continued to call for "cultural autonomy". The Walloon Movement, on the other hand, facing economic decline due to declining heavy industry, called for "socio-economic regionalism", fearing discrimination by a Belgian state dominated by the Flemish.

These two different approaches to transforming the unitary state led to Belgium's distinct form of federalism, which we can characterize as: specific, dual, egalitarian, asymmetric and unconsolidated. Another result was the disintegration of the traditional Belgian party system into two separate systems.

The split of the Belgian Socialists, Liberals and Christian-Democrats was triggered by the growing success of regionalist parties in each of the three regions, all calling for different forms of devolution. Party system fragmentation was increased by the emergence of a Flemish and Francophone ecologist (or Green) party, and a xenophobic, right-of-centre separatist party in Flanders. Hence, since the end of the 1970s, the support of 4 to 6 parties is needed to form a viable federal government, which often results in unsatisfying compromises.

> In case of conflicts between levels, these coalitions tend to defend the position only of the level at which they govern. Previously, government parties usually managed to find intraparty compromises.

Coordination between the federal and regional/community governments has also become more problematic. While until 2003, government coalitions at the constituent unit level always had the same party composition as at the federal level, now we find more and more parties that are in a regional government, but not in the federal (and vice versa). In case of conflicts between levels, these coalitions tend to defend the position only of the level at which they govern. Previously, government parties usually managed to find intraparty compromises.

Hence, our round table focused on how Belgian parties cope with the problem of coordination.

While all parties are region/community specific, they act and compete in multiple arenas (federal, regional, community, etc). Most of their political personnel (MPs, ministers) are only active at one specific level of government and develop diverging or even incongruent policy preferences that their parties have to accommodate within their own ranks.

One of the key findings of our roundtable is that this intraparty coordination occurs during weekly "party summits" that include only a very select number of the party elite, such as the party president, the head of the party research centre, the key minister(s) (often the (vice-PM) a party has at different levels and sometimes leaders of the parliamentary groups.

For the most delicate problems, an even smaller ad hoc group tends to make the decisions. There is little interparty coordination between the parties that belong to the same party family. This seems especially weak for the Flemish and Francophone Christian-Democrats, the party family present in most federal and regional/community governments.

Also Belgian civil society has its peculiarities, displaying many traces of the "consociational model" based on three "pillars" — Catholic , Socialist and Liberal — which have framed citizens' lives "from the cradle to the grave", including schools, hospitals, mutual health insurance company, trade unions, youth, women, cultural movements and newspapers. Although the three traditional parties act as representatives of these often antagonistic "ideological worlds", the Belgian consensus model is based on bargaining and cooperation between the elites of these pillars.

Hence, civil society is mostly made up of the partners of what we might call institutionalized "corporatist" negotiations, such as those between trade unions and employers associations, and those between institutionalized actors in other policy sectors, such as public health and education. Most of these partners have maintained close links to political parties.

Second, we find many new social movements mobilising around non-economic issues. While these organisations count fewer members, are less consolidated and are usually not associated with the "pillars" and the traditional parties, they are consulted (or even, at times, participate in decisions) in the sectors relevant to them. This is achieved through complex permanent formal networks of legally established committees, round table conferences and similar entities.

With the ongoing and huge policy transfers from the central government to the regions/communities, most civil society organizations have transformed their hitherto unitary model into a federal type of organization, with either Flemish and Francophone wings, or three regional branches (and often a common research center). Given the grass-roots origins of new social movements, most of them have not adopted a federal organization model. However, region and community based autonomous organizations do cooperate in public consultations.

Finally, parties tend to increasingly transform any federal policy issue into a community conflict. Any federal measure is likely to have divergent effects on different regions/communities given their socio-economic differences. A sign of this regional/community focus is the fact that in the last regional elections separatist parties captured 35 per cent of the Flemish vote! Large civil society organizations usually tend to moderate community conflicts, even when they may be also internally divided.

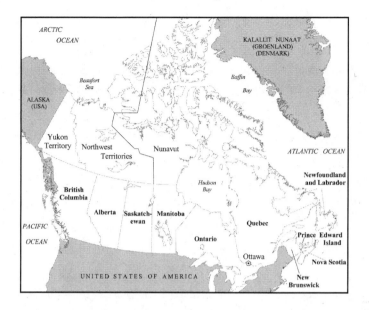

# Political Parties and Civil Society in Canada

## WILLIAM CROSS

Canada's principal political parties have long been described as playing a brokerage or aggregative function. Charged with bringing together disparate interests, representing different sides of regional and linguistic cleavages, one of the primary functions of Canadian parties has been the building of national accommodations across these divides. Today, there are two factors that challenge the ongoing ability of parties to succeed in this capacity. The first is the lack of strong vertical integration between the municipal, provincial and federal levels in the party system; and the second is a change in democratic norms, resulting in less acceptance of elites reaching accommodations combined with rising demands for direct, individual participation in party decision making.

The organization of political parties in Canada differs from that in many other federal countries due to the considerable diversity in the coordination of party activity and in party presence and organization across jurisdictions (i.e., across provincial and, even, municipal, boundaries). For example, the governing Liberal party in the province of British Columbia has little in common with the federal Liberal party in terms of ideology, organization, resources and personnel. Indeed a senior figure in the current federal Liberal party is a former British Columbia premier who led the provincial New Democratic Party, and that is not particularly exceptional.

In its current incarnation, the federal Conservative Party of Canada has no formal ties with any provincial parties. This is, in part, a result of the fact that the current federal Conservatives were formed through a merger of the "traditional" Progressive Conservatives and the Canadian Alliance, a successor group to the much more "upstart" Reform movement (see below). The natural provincial affiliations for federal Conservative activists are varied. They range from provincial Liberal parties to Progressive Conservative parties in other provinces to the small-Conservative Saskatchewan Party and Action Democratic du Quebec.

This fragmentation is further complicated by a lack of coherent party systems at the municipal level. In the vast majority of municipalities there are no formal 'party politics'. Instead, candidates run independently of any party label. In cities where municipal political parties do exist, such as Vancouver and Montreal, they have different names, identities and organizations than their provincial and federal counterparts.

This diversity and multiplicity in party systems poses challenges for civil society actors wishing to interact with and influence political parties. With little consistency to party brands, activists in civil society must attempt to influence parties at all levels of the political system, which requires expending considerable resources.

The emergence of internal party democracy, centered around individuals rather than communities, poses another challenge for the "nation building" function that political parties used to accomplish through the "brokerage" tradition. Some scholars have referred to this as the rise of 'plebiscitary' democracy within parties. In the 1990s, this approach was championed by the newly-formed, right-of-centre Reform Party. This populist and Western Canada-based political movement elected no candidates in its first federal election in 1988. By the mid-1990s, however, it had over sixty Members of Parliament (almost all from the four western provinces) and formed the official opposition. The Reform Party made great advances with voters by arguing that the "old-line" parties were elite dominated, while Reform offered all of its "grass roots" members a direct say in matters such as policy determination.

> Many suggest that these two democratic impulses — one aimed at building a national consensus and the other at individual-based democracy — are not easily combined and that they present a great challenge to Canada's parties.

The success of Reform's populist approach prompted other parties to adopt similar changes in areas such as leadership selection. Most parties today select their leader through a universal ballot of their members. This furthers the democratic tenet of one person one vote, but it does little to facilitate dialogue and accommodation across regional and linguistic divides that might occur at national conventions which bring together party members from different parts of the country. Many suggest that these two democratic impulses —

one aimed at building a national consensus and the other at individual-based democracy — are not easily combined and that they present a great challenge to Canada's parties.

In terms of the organization of civil society and whether a 'federal political culture' permeates it, there is uncertainty as to what such a political culture should look like in the Canadian case.

Given the regional and linguistic differences in the country, should civil society groups attempt to build bridges across these differences through unified national organizations, or should we expect separate organizations to arise, particularly along linguistic divides, reflecting a federal culture that respects the diversity of these different societies? There is no easy answer to this question.

The fact that a majority of Canadians are unilingual results in significant divides between Francophone and Anglophone civil society bodies. In fact, for many issue areas we find distinct civil society organizations for Francophones and Anglophones — or, sometimes, for majority-Francophone Quebec and majority-Anglophone "rest of Canada". Regardless of whether one thinks this is inherent to the Canadian federal model, this sort of schism — which means there is frequently no pan-Canadian advocacy group on an issue — poses challenges for civil society in its efforts to influence government.

The multiplicity of governmental access points offered through the federal system provides civil society with increased opportunity to connect with government and attempt to influence policy outcomes; however, the lack of 'water tight' policy compartments can make this a complicated task, as it results in overlapping jurisdiction between provincial and federal governments.

For example, a citizens' group interested in climate change needs to concern itself with the actions of all three levels of government right across the country. The federal government plays a key role in determining Canada's position on international agreements such as the Kyoto Protocol. At the same time, provincial governments exercise considerable authority over policy fields key to the Protocol's implementation, such as transportation, agriculture and energy. Further, municipal governments are responsible for the implementation and delivery of many of these policies. There is often little opportunity for inter-provincial policy coordination — the result being that patchworks of policies are likely to emerge that require civil society actors to work on many different fronts.

Finally, the traditional structures of Canadian federalism, centered on region and language, are strained by the changing nature of Canadian society.

In recent decades Canada has become increasingly diverse, with hundreds of thousands of new citizens arriving each year, largely from non-European countries. For these new Canadians the 'old' issues, defined along French/English and East/West divides, have little resonance. One of the great challenges of Canadian federalism is to bring these new Canadians, as well as Canada's founding Aboriginal peoples, fully into its democratic family and to enhance democratic practices and institutions that speak to their aspirations.

# Germany:
# A Federal Party Democracy in Transition

KLAUS DETTERBECK / WOLFGANG RENZSCH

Germany has long been a textbook model of a federal party democracy. Working within a rather homogenous political culture, parties have developed common programmatic positions shared by both federal and regional party units. Class and religion rather than territory have provided the major cleavage lines in civil society. As cohesive political blocs across the territorial levels, German parties shaped federal processes and strengthened national integration. Party competition at both the *Länder* and federal level were concentrated on a small number of parties and has been strongly congruent across the levels.

More recent challenges, however, have called into question this traditional mode of federal party politics in Germany. In particular, German reunification and European integration have led to a growth of socio-cultural, economic and political diversity. The adaptation of the German parties to this new environment will be of crucial importance for the future of German federalism.

In the postwar period, German political parties have acquired a crucial role in coordinating federal policies. German parties have developed as multi-layered and vertically integrated organizations. All major parties,

except the Bavarian Christian Social Union ( the CSU, which is closely linked
to its country-wide sister, the Christian Democratic Union, the CDU), are
present throughout Germany and seek parliamentary representation in all
parts of the country. Strong linkages between the national and the constituent
unit parties have allowed them to solve federal political conflict inside
the parties.

Cooperative federalism has worked because German parties provided
internal mechanisms to bring the various regional interests together. On
the other hand, party linkages have also been used by federal opposition
parties to restrict the powers of the federal government by employing the
veto rights of the second chamber, the *Bundesrat*. In the combination of
both dynamics, the development of the German federal system has been
closely linked to party politics.

A remarkable feature of federal party politics in Germany has been a
process of convergence of formerly diverse organizational models between
the major parties. Since the 1960s, the Social Democrats (SPD) increasingly
sought to accommodate a centralist party ethos, on one side, with pres-
sures for internal decentralization. At the same time, the party has sought
to transfer organizational power from the traditional intermediate party
level, the smaller party districts (Bezirke), to the larger *Land* parties.

For the Christian Democrats (CDU), established after 1945, the situation
was different. According to the federal ethos of "subsidiarity", the *Land*
parties developed with considerable organizational and programmatic
heterogeneity. The federal party organization, formed only in 1950, remained
weak until the early 1970s, when party reforms strengthened the federal
party executive and party headquarters. Hence, there has been a compelling
logic of adapting party organizations to the territorial structures of the
federal system. Yet, still today, the CDU *Land* party branches are somehow
more autonomous than their SPD counterparts, and enjoy a more formalized
access to the federal party executive bodies.

German federalism after 1949 has been characterized by an increasing
trend towards more cooperation and interdependence between the federal
and the constituent unit level. The sixteen *Länder* have gained their political
strength primarily from participating in federal politics via the *Bundesrat*,
and from administering federal laws. The capacity of the *Länder* for
autonomous policy making has become restricted to a few policy areas,
such as education, culture and the media. Even in these domains, however,
horizontal cooperation between the *Länder* has often accompanied regional
self-rule.

The rather "unitary" style of German federalism has to be understood in
its societal context. Lacking a strong sense of regional cultural distinctive-
ness and political cleavages on a territorial basis, German elites and the
larger citizenry have long tended to mistrust the virtues of federal policy
diversity. Former regional differences have been eroded in the post-war

period by the combined effects of: social and geographical mobility, the federal welfare state and a political system committed to the "equality of living conditions" (Article 72,2 Basic Law). While regionalist parties have not played a significant role, country-wide parties and civil society groups — organized along federal lines with integrated regional branches — were characterized by a rather strong orientation towards the national level as they sought uniform solutions to political problems.

However, federal party democracy is currently in a transition period. Following long debates, federal constitutional reforms have been enacted which aim at strengthening the legislative and fiscal autonomy of the *Länder*. While these reforms fall short of a radical departure from the cooperative path, they signify the willingness among German political elites to accept stronger competitive elements in federalism.

With respect to the social context, the most outstanding development is the divide in economic development and political culture between West and East Germany, following reunification in 1990. Most importantly, East Germans more strongly emphasize the role of the state in welfare provision and employment as a result of both socialist experiences and the specific problems of higher unemployment and economic transformation in the East.

> Federal constitutional reforms have been enacted which aim at strengthening the legislative and fiscal autonomy of the *Länder*. While these reforms fall short of a radical departure from the cooperative path, they signify the willingness among German political elites to accept stronger competitive elements in federalism.

There are also significant elements of change with respect to party competition. First of all, regional patterns have become more distinct since 1990. While there had already been variations to the regional strengths of German parties before reunification, there is now a rather clear divide between East and West Germany with respect to the political relevance of the smaller parties. The post-socialist Party of Democratic Socialism — the former Communists, now called "The Left" — has become a major player in the East, while remaining marginal or a rather small player in the West. By contrast, the Greens and the "liberal" Free Democratic Party were absent from Eastern *Länder* through most of the 1990s.

Second, the balance between federal and regional issues in *Land* elections has shifted to some extent. With *Land* policies becoming more relevant by the effects of federal reform and the European single market, regional party branches and regional voters tend to focus their attention more strongly on regional issues and candidates. While socio-economic policies still tend to dominate *Land* elections, they are now more often framed in a regional rather than national terms. Yet, federal politics and the popularity of the national government still play an important role in German *Land* elections.

Third, government formation for both the *Länder* and the federal government has become more complex. Over the last few years, there has been a trend towards having five or six parties represented in the parliaments, with pronounced regional differences in party strength. It has therefore become much more difficult to model *Land* coalitions on federal patterns. We see a strong heterogeneity in regional government formations, with parties increasingly willing to have different partners in different places, at the same time. As a result, majority building in the *Bundesrat* has become a more difficult task. This may lead to a situation where *Land* interests rather than party allegiances more strongly determine *Land* government action in the second chamber.

As a result of all these changes, the role of German political parties in promoting national integration has come under pressure. *Land* party branches are more strongly confronted with distinct patterns of regional party competition. When using their formal powers to go their own ways — in terms of electoral campaigning, policy programs and coalition-building — the territorial levels of parties will tend to become less cohesive. More decentralized parties, however, will find it difficult to govern within Germany's "interlocked" federal system. Therefore, there is room for change, both to the German federal system and for German political parties.

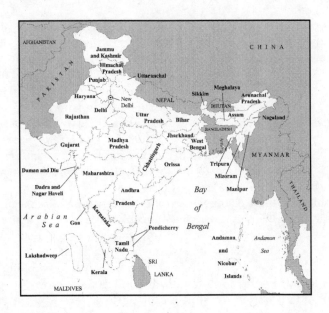

# Political Parties and Civil Society Organizations in the Federal Democratic Process in India

SANDEEP SHASTRI

The Indian polity of today can best be described as a federal democratic process involving multi-party competition and an emerging civil society network at the local level. The role and position that political parties and civil society organizations have come to play in the Indian political system is closely linked to both the consolidation of democratic processes and the dynamics of federal politics over the last few decades.

The democratic and federal context in which political parties operate and civil society organizations function provides a revealing perspective for an analysis of their comparative roles and their influence over the nature and course of Indian politics.

A survey of the working of Indian democracy in the six decades since independence indicates certain trends that have important implications for the cut and thrust of political party organization and politics. Taken together, the strengthening of democratic processes and the deepening of democratic practices have pushed political parties and other forms of civic organizations to the centre-stage. When the nation began its journey after independence, and sought to stabilize its democratic institutions and processes, the need of the hour was to ensure greater national integration and a politics of consensus. This had a clear and direct impact on the working of political parties. Additionally, the fact of a first-past-the-post (FPTP) electoral system also had an impact on the nature and structure of party competition. While a federal structure was put in place, in the constitutional design of the polity, it placed a premium on the role of the Union or federal government. All these factors contributed, at that time, to the polity gravitating towards a one party dominant system.

Six decades of democratic politics with free, fair and competitive elections, and growing assertion of the rights of the states, has significantly altered the political landscape and the framework of party politics and competition. Political and social identities have increasingly asserted themselves at the regional level and are now authentically articulated in the politics of the states. Successive elections have seen competition focused on politics at the state level.

With the passage of time, the states of India have emerged as the nodal point of political contestation. A natural corollary is the increasing focus of party organizations at the state level. The weakening of the one party dominant system was first seen in the Indian states and then gathered momentum at the national level. The accordance of constitutional status to increasingly strong local government institutions has further deepened democratic politics in India. The implications of these developments for both political parties and civil society organizations are far reaching.

The expanding base of democratic participation has created both challenges as well as opportunities for political parties. In the days of the one party dominant framework, the Indian National Congress (INC) projected itself as the "catch-all" party of national unity and integration. After exercising a near monopoly over power at the state level for the first two decades after independence, and at national level for the first three decades, Congress has seen a gradual collapse of the social coalition it had built up. It has been forced to concede power in many states to its political rivals, many of which were splinter groups of Congress.

However, Congress continued to be the major political player until the late 1980s. It is the 1990s which saw the clear emergence of a competitive multi-party system. Since the mid 1990s, the country has seen only coalition governments (relatively stable over the last fifteen years) at the national level. This trend is a clear signal of the end of one-party domination and the emergence of a genuinely competitive multi-party system.

The dynamics of federalism have left their clear footprints on the working of the party system. A trend that is gaining ascendancy since the 1980s is the sharp rise in the number of state based parties represented both in the national (federal or Union) parliament and in the state legislatures. The rise of political parties whose support base is limited to a single or a few states is now a common phenomenon. Many now question the status of the national parties, as recognized by the Election Commission, on the ground that these parties often do not have a genuinely national presence, either in terms of their votes share or from the perspective of the spread of seats that they win in elected legislative bodies. Many would prefer to change the label from "national" parties to "multi-state" parties in view of this new trend.

Yet another feature of the Indian party system is the increasing fragmentation of political parties. All the major political parties have witnessed a number of splits during their life time. Many of the state-based parties of today are splinter groups that emerged from either national parties or other state-based parties.

One factor that has triggered this process is a lack of internal democracy in political parties. Competitive elections for positions are absent in most political parties. Parties' preference, as a rule, is to choose the route of nomination by the High Command or central leadership of the party. This often results in a significant measure of dissent, which leads to splitting of parties.

A linked factor is the powerful influence of the personality of individual leaders in shaping the political destinies of parties. The emergence of powerful political dynasties across the political spectrum is a natural by-product of the influence of personality.

The top-down structure of party organization has stifled the internal democratic process in most political parties. It has also weakened grass-roots level organization of parties. More often than not, it is difficult to clearly perceive any party structures lower than the district or sub-state level. Loyalty beyond this point is more often to party leaders rather than political parties.

Civil society organizations have been operating in India for quite some time, in a few select domains. In the area of coordinating the delivery of public services and protection of citizens' rights, several civil society organizations have operated throughout the country. In recent years, the media has focused on the role of civil society groups in drawing attention to problems faced by ordinary citizens, in ensuring efficiency in service delivery and in advocating for the protection of basic rights. A conscious trend in the civil society movement is to adopt a distinctly apolitical stance. In many cases, civil society organizations have sought to portray their activities as an alternative to mainstream politics. This has often placed them at cross purposes with political parties. Further, given the fluidity of party organizations at the local level, civil society organizations have frequently stepped in to discharge the "interest-articulation" function that local party units might normally expected to perform.

The evolving nature and functioning of political parties clearly demonstrates the impact of critical changes in the workings of India's democracy and federal system over the past two decades. The "federalizing of democracy" and the "democratization of federalism" have resulted in the emergence of a new typology of political parties. Political parties are no longer seen as either national or regional but more as either multi–state or single-state. The polity has clearly moved from being a one-party dominant system to a competitive multi party system.

Given the fact that there is no comprehensive legislation to regulate the organization and functioning of political parties in India, they are marked by a near absence of internal democracy and are prone to intense factionalism and frequent splitting. Political dynasties seem to play a preeminent role across parties, causing increasing public frustration with all political parties. Successive surveys of trust in public institutions have placed political parties very low in the esteem of the Indian population.

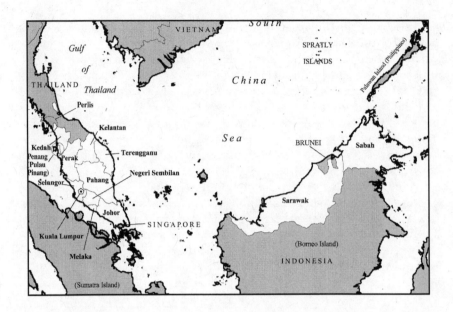

# Recent Social and Political Changes
# Augurs Well for the Restructuring
# of Malaysia's Federalism

## FRANCIS KOK WAH LOH

These are heady days in Malaysian politics. A breakthrough by the Opposition in the 2008 polls has set in motion the transformation of the one dominant party system — which had been in place since Independence in 1957 — into a competitive, two-party system. In tandem with this, a shift from a centralized to a more cooperative federalism is also underway.

In the 12th Malaysian General Election, held on March 8, 2008, the National Front (BN) ruling coalition was returned to power. However, it failed to secure its usual two-thirds majority, the threshold that it counts as a successful electoral outing and that allows it to amend the Constitution at will — something it has resorted to more than 60 times. Hence the National Front's simple majority victory could be viewed as a failure of sorts.

The National Front was also defeated in an unprecedented five out of thirteen state legislatures. These included Selangor and Penang, the two most industrialized states in the Peninsula, as well as the northern states of Perak, Kedah and Kelantan, which together produce most of the country's rice. And so, the 2008 polls also signaled an important shift in the balance of power between Kuala Lumpur and the constituent states, and, potentially, a restructuring of Malaysia's centralized federal system.

The National Front is led by the United Malays National Organization (UMNO) and includes the Malaysian Chinese Association (MCA) and the Malaysian Indian Congress (MIC). Prior to 2008, it had lost its two-thirds majority only once, in the 1969 election. Race riots after that historic watershed led to radical changes:

- the introduction of the affirmative-action New Economic Policy (NEP, 1971-1990) favouring the poorer Malay majority;
- the expansion of the three member coalition to the present-day 14-party National Front coalition; and
- the passing of anti-democratic constitutional amendments including the tightening of an anti-sedition law, ostensibly to curb racial tensions.

With these developments, the opposition was virtually snuffed out while UMNO's pre-eminence was consolidated.

Thanks to the discovery of petroleum resources in the 1970s, a commodities boom from mid-1970s to mid-1990s and increased levels of foreign direct investments following the Plaza Accords in 1985, Malaysia experienced rapid industrialization and economic growth while fulfilling NEP goals. However, by the time of the 1997-98 regional financial crisis, Malaysia's political economy was also characterized by creeping cronyism, due to the NEP.

That said, economic growth and the NEP also led to the emergence of a multi-ethnic business and middle-class, transforming Malaysian society in the process. In turn, the middle-class contributed to the formation of new interest groups, non-governmental organizations (NGOs), new parties and, ultimately, a new opposition coalition.

As in other countries in the region undergoing similar socio-economic transformation, some segments of the middle-class called for democratic reform and for accountability and transparency in government to curb cronyism. Ultimately, those segments also resorted to electoral politics to challenge the BN's stranglehold on parliament. By the 1990s, a more fragmented politics, not simply one organized along ethnic lines, emerged. The BN advantage was its ability to count on its 14 component parties to mobilize cross-ethnic support while the opposition tended to mobilize along mono-ethnic lines.

All this changed in 2008. A solid swing among ethnic Indian voters, traditionally pro-BN, was accompanied by an equally pronounced switch of ethnic Chinese voters to the opposition. Both dovetailed with a shift among ethnic Malays for a new party, the People's Justice Party (PKR).

The PKR's campaign was led by the charismatic Anwar Ibrahim, previously deputy Prime Minister and UMNO's deputy president. He had reimmersed himself in Malaysian politics after two-plus years' incarceration on trumped-up charges of sodomy and abuse of powers when deputy PM. Under Ibrahim's leadership, the PKR developed into the opposition party of the centre, forging alliances with the Islamic Party of Malaysia (Pas) which contested in rural ethnic Malay seats, and the Democratic Action Party (DAP) which contested in urban ethnic Chinese seats. The upshot: an unexpected swing away from the BN towards a new multi-ethnic opposition coalition called Pakatan Rakyat (PR) comprising the PKR, DAP and Pas.

Wider issues were also responsible for the winds of change. Ethnic Indian anger at that groups's economic and political marginalization had manifested itself in a massive demonstration in Kuala Lumpur in November 2007, organized by a new group called Hindu Rights Action Front ("Hindraf"). The ethnic Chinese were unhappy with the sluggish economy and the inability of the BN government to improve Malaysia's competitiveness regionally. Some argue that this was due, in part, to the NEP.

Inflation also contributed to the electoral outcome. The hike in fuel prices had resulted in a higher cost of living which had a great impact on the poor and middle-class of all races. Others were concerned about rising crime rates, corruption and abuses by BN leaders, especially in the local councils and state governments. Exposés of some of these follies were posted in the electronic media, on websites and blogs, though they went unreported in the mainstream media, largely owned or controlled by BN parties.

In essence, a large percentage of the middle-class — and to some extent even the business class — was in revolt. Their complaints were largely urban middle-class concerns, which perhaps explains why the more developed states of Penang, Selangor and Perak, as well as in the Federal Territory of Kuala Lumpur fell to the opposition in the 2008 polls.

The BN coalition no longer dominates Malaysian politics as before. The transformation of Malaysia's one dominant party system to a competitive two-party system is underway. More than that, the opposition PR-led states have demanded additional funds for development projects and — by means of new laws and policies at the state level — are undermining Malaysia's centralized federalism. For instance, documents on failed development projects carried out by previous BN state governments, though classified as 'Official Secrets' under federal law, have been declassified by the PR-led governments, exposing alleged corruption and malpractice. Furthermore, the Selangor state goverment is in the process of legislating its own Freedom of Information Act, while in Penang, the PR-led government passed a resolution calling for the restoration of local authority elections, which the BN federal government had abolished in the early 1970s.

The federal government has also resorted to measures deemed 'undemocratic' by the PR-led governments, to "recapture" the Perak state government by persuading three state assemblypersons to cross the floor.

The standoff between the PR-state governments and the BN federal government has encouraged the BN-led state governments of Sabah and Sarawak, among the poorest in the federation, to press for new concessions for their states: more federal cabinet positions, increased development allocations, greater autonomy in determining their affairs and selecting state leaders, etc. What this means is that a secondary effect of the 2008 polls could be a restructuring of federal-state relations in Malaysia.

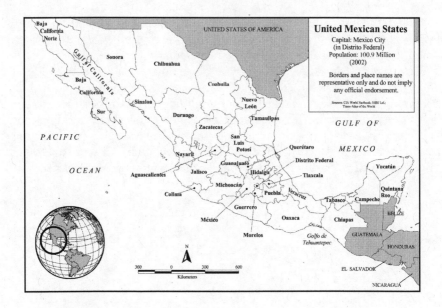

**United Mexican States**

Capital: Mexico City
(in Distrito Federal)
Population: 100.9 Million
(2002)

Borders and place names are
representative only and do not imply
any official endorsement.

Sources: CIA World Factbook; ESRI Ltd.;
Times Atlas of the World.

# Federalism, Political Parties
# and Civil Society in Mexico

JEAN-FRANÇOIS PRUD'HOMME

To talk about the relationship between federalism, political parties and civil society in Mexico means talking about regime change and democratization. In July 2000, after more than seventy years of government by a dominant party, the *Partido Revolucionario Institucional* (PRI), an opposition candidate, Vicente Fox from the *Partido Acción Nacional* (PAN), won the presidential election. For many political analysts, the election meant a turning point in a long process of democratic transition. From that point onwards, Mexico's political system was more plural and has had to adapt its institutions and practices to democratic norms. This adaptation process naturally included the workings of the federal system.

Mexico is an old federation. Its first Constitution (1824) adopted a federal system. With the exception of a short unitary interlude (1836-1857), all the subsequent constitutions included federal provisions.

In spite of this long legal tradition, authentic federal practices are new in Mexico. In effect, for most of the nineteenth century the country was prey to instability and political turmoil. Under the dictatorship of Porfirio Díaz (1877-1911), the central government consolidated its authority to the detriment of local and state governments, and the same story was repeated after the Revolution. After a few decades of centralization of authority at the hands of the central executive branch, the federal provisions became more a constitutional myth than a reality.

One of the peculiarities of the authoritarian regime that consolidated after the Mexican revolution lay in what became to be known as the *meta-constitutional powers* of the president. As the virtual head of the dominant party, the president exerted political control over the other branches of government (legislative and judicial) as well the state and local levels of government. It suffices to mention that from 1917 until the end of PRI domination in the twenty-first century, 61 governors were actually removed by presidents who made use of a constitutional disposition related to the "disappearance of powers". Whenever there was a controversy between the states and the federal governments, the presidents could use their formal and informal powers to replace annoying governors. It should also be stressed that it was not until 1989 that the federal government officially recognized an opposition candidate victory in a state election for governorship (Baja California, PAN).

The electoral laws and the configuration of the party system were instrumental in increasing the central government's control over constituent unit level politics. The hegemonic party system that consolidated after 1946 allowed for a certain level of pluralism side-by-side with government control on the nature and influence of the opposition parties. Mexican law required that political parties satisfy a number of conditions in order to be registered as official parties. Among those conditions, they had to certify that they were "national parties" with members in two-thirds of the national territory. Until the 1980s, the PRI candidates used to win elections with a landslide while the victories of opposition parties were very scarce. Their representation in Congress was limited, first, to "party deputies" and, later, to proportional representation deputies. In other words, the PRI controlled political representation.

Intergovernmental affairs were essentially a matter of governing party internal affairs. There were strong disincentives for the creation of regional parties, and opposition political representation was virtually without a territorial basis. Obviously, the combination of those elements did not help to promote a vigorous practice of federal governance. As for civil society, the PRI was dominant here as well. Grassroots activities of the post revolutionary years were channeled nation-wide through a corporatist integration with the governing party of unions, peasant organizations and, later, middle class associations. In fact, these unions, associations and organizations were the backbones of the three "sectors" of the PRI. In addition, entrepreneurs were encouraged to organize in big national organizations. Negotiations between civil society actors and the government were conducted along vertical corporatist lines.

Democratic transition took place against that background. The territorial dimension was very important in the process – for at least two reasons. First, in the negotiations over the democratization of the political system, the government was willing to cede ground at the local level in order to maintain its control on the central government. So, the opposition parties started to concentrate their efforts at winning local and state governments in order to eventually conquer the national government. Second, the financial and fiscal crisis of the 1980's led the central government to decentralize the administration of public resources through the strengthening of municipal governments and the transfer of administrative capacities to state governments (health and education). The combination of these factors created the perception that democracy and active federalism were closely related. That was partially true, although the relationship was hardly a given.

The territorial focus of the opposition parties was quite successful. In 2000, when the PAN candidate won the presidential election, his party was governing nine states and the other big opposition party, the *Partido de la Revolution Democratic* (PRD), was governing five states including the Federal District, leaving 18 states in the hands of the PRI. Furthermore, the access to power of a non-PRI president had the immediate effect of breaking what was left of the political networks that sustained the *metaconstitutionnal powers* of the president. Pluralism and the relaxation of central government control created a perfect scenario for the reactivation of federalism. The federal principles of the constitution were not going to be lettres mortes anymore. As a matter of fact, in 2001, governors from the PRD and the PRI (in its new role as an opposition party) created the National Conference of Governors (CONAGO) to negotiate with the federal government. They were later joined by PAN's governors. However, many of those who were expecting the beginning of a new intergovernmental politics were disillusioned. It requires time to consolidate new institutions and practices.

Even if there was a pre-existing constitutional framework for the practice of federalism, there was no model for its implementation. The main political actors involved in the process of intergovernmental politics had to invent new political practices of cooperation and negotiation. Soon, it became clear that they did not necessarily share a common definition of what they wanted to gain in their negotiations with the federal government.

If, in general terms, it could be said that the governors wanted more fiscal resources, they did not have a clear and shared vision of the objectives, mechanisms and general workings of the new federal system. The differences in the size, wealth and capacity of the 32 federal entities (31 states and the Federal District) contributed to the difficulty of imagining the workings of federalism in a new democratic context.

As well, in the same way that it happened in other venues of public policy, the new context of pluralism and democracy allowed for petty politics to creep into intergovernmental politics. In the Mexican national party system, local and state politics are closely connected to the federal arena. The electoral calendar tends to be loaded with local, state and mid-term elections and the results of each are perceived as measures of the *rapport de force* among the main national parties. Short-term visions prevail in the policy-making process, making cooperation on fundamental issues between the main political actors difficult. We have seen the same phenomenon in the federal legislative arena since 2000.

Finally, the meaning of the association between active federalism and democracy has changed. During the period of transition to democracy, the association between local and state autonomy and democracy was highly positive. After all, it was at the sub-national levels of government that the opposition parties could show how democratic governments could offer more effective governance. Now, however, local and state autonomy is frequently associated with the persistence of authoritarianism. It does not help that, in general, democratic reform has not followed the same pace at the federal and sub-national levels of government, especially when it comes to accountability and transparency in the management of public finances. Governors have also acquired more autonomy and political influence during the last ten years; and there is a general perception that they are less subject to social and political control than the federal politicians.

The national party system tends to give a national dimension to local and regional politics; but it frequently does so through of the involvement of local elites, without contributing to the democratization of local politics. This may be a reflection of the state of the national parties, and it is surely a reflection of the unequal development of civil society in Mexico. The re-activation of a strong federalism requires the strengthening of civil society and the institutionalization of the party system at the local and state level.

In sum, in the context of a discussion on federalism, political parties and civil society the Mexican case shows how federal systems can affect and interact with the process of democratic change. The current state of the Mexican federal system shows the enormous progress accomplished in terms of democratization over the past twenty-five years; but there is no inherent or necessary association between federalism and democracy. Moreover, as in other arenas of the public sphere, Mexico faces the challenges of institution-building and the adoption of new practices. This state of affairs is, without a doubt, "interesting" for a country that is, after all, an old federation.

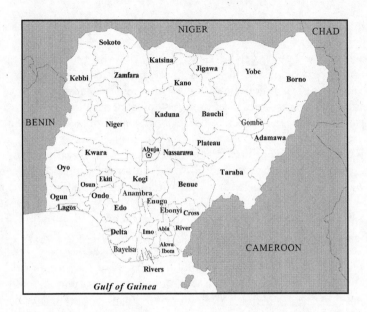

# How Relevant Are Political Parties
# and Civil Society to the Evolution
# of Federalism in Nigeria?

JIBRIN IBRAHIM / OKON AKIBA

Nigeria is one of the world's largest federal democratic experiments. Located on the south-eastern flank of West Africa, its population of over 140 million is composed of roughly 350 ethnic groups, with three dominant ones making up 60 percent of the total: the Hausa (north and northwest, 28 percent); the Yoruba (southwest, 18 percent), and the Igbo (southeast, 14 percent). There are hundreds of other culturally-defined identities, among them the Fulani, Kanuri, Nupe, and Tiv in the north; and the Ibibio, Ijaw, Edo, Urhobo, and Efik in the south.

Given this size and diversity, it is not surprising that Nigerians have two political principles to which they are committed: federalism and democracy.

The Nigerian people's historic experience with both has, however, been tortuous. It was the Sardauna of Sokoto, leader of the Northern Peoples' Congress (NPC) in the colonial period and during the early days of Nigerian independence, who first referred to the amalgamation of the Nigerian provinces as "the mistake of 1914". That was in the early 1950s, when the Sardauna had to accommodate his southern colleagues on the terms of independence and federalism. The Sardauna's Northern Peoples' Congress inherited power from the British at independence as the ruling party both in the (largest) Northern Region and at the federal level. The opposition was led by the Action Group which was dominated by Yoruba and which controlled the Western Region. The Eastern Region was under the control of the Igbos and their party, the National Council of Nigeria and the Cameroons (NCNC).

This problematic mix of powerful ethno-regional political parties shaping the character of both the struggle for independence and the practice of Nigerian federalism created tensions that have marked the country's politics ever since. The most tragic and wrenching event in this regard was the civil war of 1967 to 1970, which posed a serious threat to the existence of Nigeria as a country and caused the loss of over a million lives.

Tense civil and communal relations dominated the first phase of Nigerian federalism, from 1958 to 1965. It was a period characterized by the political mobilization of ethno-regional identities, with the objective of gaining access to regional power. At that time, the real locus of power was in the regions, as the number of national elites was relatively small. Federal power was, however, still significant and the powerful elite in the regions fought among themselves for what came to be known as the "national cake".

The civil war from 1967 to 1970 was, in effect, a bloody and brutal way to resolve the inter-ethnic and elite conflicts that had marked the first period of Nigeria's independence. The end of that conflagration resulted, for a considerable period, in military dictatorship and a *de-facto* unitary state. This regime (or, more precisely, series of military regimes) signalled a diminution of the key role of ethno-regional identities had played Nigerian politics and the consequent weakening of regional bases of power. The sole goal of political mobilization became the conquest of federal power at the centre. This transformation was, literally, fuelled by a vast increase in the federal government's revenues from petroleum resources.

Over the past four decades, the Nigerian state has evolved from a federal polity characterised by three politically strong regions, each controlled by the elite of a majority ethnic group — Hausa, Yoruba and Igbo — to a highly centralized system. Currently, the 36 so-called federated states have no real autonomous powers and are at the beck and call of a strong centre. Enormous powers are vested in the hands of one person, and in one institution: the president and the presidency. This political transformation was carried out mainly under military rule in a context in which excessive corruption and primordial issues of ethnic, religious and regional political domination have become central elements in the country's political culture.

Ethno-regional identities have become problematic in Nigeria because they have been associated with perceptions of discrimination against some groups, and the inability of those groups to gain access to wealth and the levers of power. The main issues have been control of the armed forces, of the judiciary and of government bureaucracy.

The shift of power from the regions to the centre has weakened the role of political parties in Nigerian federalism. Regional and ethnic parties have been constitutionally outlawed. Ethno-regionalism is now accommodated through what is described as the "zoning system", in which government offices are rotated to Nigerians from different ethno-regional groups.

The original deformity of Nigerian political parties was that they lacked an ideology for nation building, were parochial organizations whose leaders trenchantly rejected cross-regional alliances, and used dubious mechanisms to protect their territories against penetration by rival political parties. Internecine bloody conflicts, mutual animosities among regionally dominant political leaders, and the parties' proclivities for mobilizing society on ethnic appeals severely jeopardized the original democratic, federal experiment.

In effect, the first federal experiment proved to be unsustainable largely because of failures on the part of party leadership to build a cooperative spirit and nurture those democratic virtues considered to be essential to peace building in a federation: compromise, consensus, predisposition to negotiation, and trust.

The current federal arrangement was bequeathed to Nigeria by the military. Successive military dictatorships dismantled the parliamentary system of government in favour of an American-type presidential system, with the concentration of legislative powers at the centre, and federal control over the police force, prisons, education, the judiciary, and revenue allocation. The latter entailed abandoning the previous "derivation" principles in revenue allocation in favour of alternative, "equity-informed" principles.

In addition, the government used its right to create new states to aggrandize its own position by replacing, over time, the original three regions with 36 states. This increase in the number of states was also designed to protect the minorities in regions, eliminate secessionist impulses, and minimize violent ethnic and religious incidents.

All Nigerian federal administrations have used centralization and state creation as major mechanisms of national integration and (at least an attempt at) good governance. These integrationist concepts are entrenched and fully enunciated in Nigeria's most recent democratic and federal Constitution of 1999.

Other integrative strategies have also evolved over time: the "federal character" principle aims to ensure equal representation of Nigerian citizens in federal appointments, scholarship access, promotion in the military, and so on; and broadly based political parties are required by the constitution to have memberships that cut across ethnic and regional lines.

Far less securely embedded in federalist thought in the country is the so-called "zoning scheme", which is being proposed as a new means of cultivating national unity, through the rotation of high political offices among a cluster of ethnic groupings.

Most public officials believe that creating a multiplicity of states has eliminated secessionist impulses from the body politic and promoted a higher sense of national belonging or loyalty. However, leaders in civil society and many Nigerian intellectuals argue that the newly created states are not economically viable entities, and the cost of administering them cannot be justified. They see state creation as a drain on national resources. Advocates for reform in this regard want a return to some form of what existed during the beginnings of an independent Nigeria, when the regions controlled their resources and enjoyed greater autonomy in the exploitation and disposal of their natural wealth.

Official records show that the three regions in the Nigeria of the early 1960s were economically and financially independent. They generated roughly 50% of their own revenue and shared the collective revenues of the federation equally with the federal government. However, the rise in oil revenue and the concomitant centralization of power has seen a reversal in the fiscal balance: centrally collected oil revenue now provides roughly 80% of all public revenue and 90% of export revenues. Sharp declines in regionally controlled agricultural sales taxes are linked to an equally steep rise in the receipts of federal customs and excise taxes.

Most public officials believe that creating a multiplicity of states has eliminated secessionist impulses from the body politic and promoted a higher sense of national belonging or loyalty. However, leaders in civil society and many Nigerian intellectuals argue that the newly created states are not economically viable entities.

In Nigeria, the states are not required to function as self-sufficient units. They are supported by the distributive actions of the Federal Government. The implications of this federal control are widely debated among researchers and non-governmental organizations interested in the management of fiscal federalism. There is some truth in their arguments that revenue allocation in Nigeria is excessively politicized. True federalism, the argument goes, must encourage market-oriented competitiveness. Each constituent unit government needs to develop its own tax base and guarantees of systematic redistribution of revenues to unviable units can only encourage patronage politics, lack of transparency, conflicts over the spoils of political office and the "underdevelopment" of federalism.

Fiscal centralization has meant that the federal centre now exercises exclusive control over the distribution of all oil revenue accruing to it from the Niger Delta regions of southern Nigeria, which is then allocated back to the states based on the mixed principles of derivation, need, territorial size, and challenge of development.

Although arrangements have been initiated to hand over some control of offshore oil resources to oil producing states, public officials fear that agitation for decentralization of revenue allocation is aggravating inter-ethnic tensions. Indeed, calls for fiscal decentralization are treated, officially, as fundamentally antagonistic toward the resource poor, vulnerable northern states.

There is, however, contrary argument to the effect that federal revenue redistribution complicates ethnic relations. It generates resentment not only in resource-rich states, whose populations accuse the government of paying inadequate attention to the environmental consequences of oil production in the Niger Delta wetland, but also in resource poor northern states, who fear that their development needs might be relegated to a secondary place.

Many leaders of civil society want adjustments in Nigeria's fiscal policy — adjustments in favour of decentralization which they say will eliminate corruption, enforce discipline and accountability in the federal management of national projects, and enshrine social justice in the relationships between the federal centre and the constituent units.

Further complicating the management of federalism in Nigeria is the question of religious intolerance and demands by fundamentalist groups in the northern parts of the country for the recognition of Musilm Shari'a Law as a legal system. Despite the fact that the 1999 Nigerian Constitution, like the preceding ones, prohibits the adoption of a state religion by any of its administrative components, Shari'a advocates in many of the northern states argue that secularism is inherently biased against the Islamic faith, since Islam supports unity between state and religion.

Following the example of Zamfara state, 12 other northern states have adopted Shari'a criminal laws including the "hudud" punishments, i.e., the cutting of arms for theft, and abolition of the sale of alcohol. Mass protests by Christians against the adoption of Shari'a criminal law resulted in killings in which many of the victims have been Igbo from the east — uncomfortably echoing events that triggered the civil war in the late 1960s.

The result has been an active debate on a redefinition of Nigerian federalism. Some propose that the country adopt a confederated system that would give maximum autonomy in the control of economic and political affairs to the constituent units. The Yoruba organization, Afenifere, supports the idea of such a loose confederacy. There is similar support from a major Igbo organization, Ohaneze Ndigbo. Thinly veiled, perhaps even subliminal, it appears that the real message in the support for a confederacy is fear of increasing "Islamization" in the North and the threat of losing access to federally disbursed oil revenues.

Nigeria is confronting critical political challenges that raise serious questions about its identity and its functioning as a federal country. The rise and expansion of sectarian conflicts, the discrimination against Nigerian citizens living in states in which they do not have direct ethno-biological roots, insurgency in the oil producing Niger Delta of the south, contentious struggles over revenue sharing, agitation for reform in revenue allocation and for decentralization of the federation itself all point to the existence of strong impulses toward a new experiment based on a loose federal arrangement with a much weaker centre than the current one.

We can also see that broad coalitions of civil society organizations and hundreds of civic groups are deeply concerned about these developments. They are united in thinking that ongoing tensions and violence in society are organically linked to failures in the Nigerian government's economic policies and a lack of respect for democratic principles. Now, more than ever, it is imperative for those in control in Nigeria to pay careful attention to voices from the grass roots. Government must heed the warnings about a need to couple the current official federal focus on national integration with real and deliberate efforts toward sustaining democracy and ensuring economic progress for all citizens.

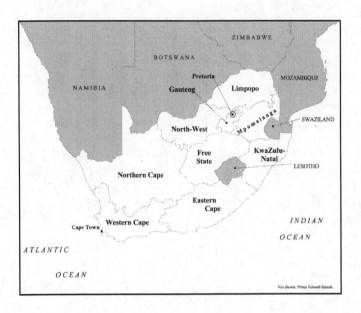

Not shown: Prince Edward Islands

# The Development of Democracy in South Africa – A Journey without a Roadmap

## CHRIS TAPSCOTT

The form of the South African state, and the political system which under-girds it, is the outcome of an agreement brokered during the multi-party negotiations which preceded the end of apartheid rule and the advent of democracy in 1994. While the predominant liberation movement led by the African National Congress (ANC) and its allies favoured a unitary state as a means to transform a highly fractured and unequal society, the representa-tives of some minority groups (and particularly those of the white population then in power) favoured a federal system as means to disperse power and, by implication, to retain greater influence in the polity. Thus, while the 1996 Constitution speaks of a single sovereign state, the three-tiered struc-ture of national, provincial and local government in place has many features of a federal system and holds the potential, over time, for a more balanced distribution of power across society. However, like many societies emerging from an extended period of autocratic rule, South Africa is still in the process of consolidating both the systems and practices of democratic governance and this is likely to be more protracted than initially anticipated.

Formally, the institutions of a democratic state are in place and a clear separation of powers is prescribed in the constitution. Having said that, the not-fully-realized mutation of the ruling ANC from a liberation movement to a formal political power in office has meant that, in practice, there is not always a clear distinction between party, government and state bureaucracy. This practice has been effectively condoned by the majority of citizens, most of whom have had no experience of living in a federal democracy and have tended to accept the status quo as normal.

Similarly, while the 1996 Constitution makes provision for a significant degree of decentralization to the provincial and local levels, it is evident that many citizens do not have a clear understanding of the distinct roles and responsibilities of the different levels of government. Public opinion surveys have also repeatedly revealed that a large proportion of the population have little trust in local government and look to the central government for their sustenance. A major component of the democratic infrastructure, as a consequence, currently lacks legitimacy.

The second chamber of the legislature, the National Council of Provinces (NCOP), makes provision for the representation of regional concerns in national policy formulation. However, the dominance of the ANC in all but one of the nine provinces, together with strong central control of the party, is such that the NCOP has thus far served largely as a rubber stamp for decisions of the national government. Notwithstanding this fact, the provinces are beginning to develop their own political dynamic and — although this has generally been shaped by race and ethnicity and, to a lesser extent, by class — it is indicative of a slow change in the configuration of national power. This was never more evident than at the 2008 ANC Convention where individual provinces voted *en bloc* for their choice of leaders and ended a hitherto unanimous election process.

Loyalty to the ruling party as the liberators of the oppressed majority, nevertheless, is such that elections have tended to be based on political identity rather than on substantive policy issues. This has also meant that individual political leaders are generally not held to account. This state of affairs is aggravated by a system of proportional representation and the fact that political constituencies have no direct say in the election of political office bearers. This has limited the prospects for opposition parties, although recent splits in the ANC, which led to the formation of the Congress of the People (COPE), and the strengthening of the official opposition, the Democratic Alliance (DA), in the 2008 election, have signaled a slight shift to a more vibrant form of multi-party democracy.

Perhaps as a consequence of the loss of the Western Cape province to the opposition, and reduced majorities in several provinces, some in the ANC have re-opened the debate on whether there remains a need for provincial government at all. Should this initiative be advanced seriously, it will provide a litmus test of the extent to which regional political groupings (particularly those within the ANC) have embraced the authority devolved to them.

Civil society in South Africa is generally weak and has thus far failed to transcend the racial, ethno-regional and sectarian cleavages which are a legacy of the divide-and-rule strategies of the Apartheid regime.

The development of civil society has also been constrained by the manner in which the ruling party has engaged with social movements and organizations. Having swept into office on a tide of popular resistance, the incoming government effectively brought the notion of citizen participation into the political mainstream and raised it to a first principle of government policy. However, it is evident that, politically, the ANC still perceives itself to be the vanguard of popular struggles and, in so doing, crowds out attempts by civil society organizations to represent popular aspirations. In this context, the independent mobilization of citizens on even the most mundane of matters is perceived in some segments of the ruling elite to be a threat to the status of elected officials and a direct challenge to the party as a whole.

Perhaps as a consequence of the ineffectiveness of civil society organizations, and frustration with the slow pace of service delivery at the local level, there was an upsurge in social protest activity during the first decade of the new millennium. Some 6,000 protests were officially recorded during the 2004-2005 financial year and an estimated fifteen protests were being held *per day* somewhere in South Africa during 2007. For many poor and disadvantaged communities, protest action coexists with, and in some instances supplants, formal institutional channels for engagement with the state over basic socio-economic rights. Should this community based-mobilization, which is generally locally-based and not continuous over time, coalesce into more formal social movement organizations (as has occurred in several instances) it holds the potential for the development of a more robust and influential civil society.

# Spain: Decentralization as a Contentious Issue in Party Competition and Public Discourse

## FRANCESC PALLARES / JAVIER ASTUDILLO

The open design of the "State of Autonomies" established by the 1978 Cons-titution has, three decades later, produced very high levels of decentra-lization. Despite the fact that the Constitution set a fast-track process to be applied in the so-called "historical" regions (namely, Catalonia, the Basque Country and Galicia) and a slow-track devolution process to be applied in the "non-historical" regions, by the late 1990s there symmetry in the distribution of responsibilities — though variance still exists with regards to fiscal autonomy.

The initial asymmetric design of the devolution process set in motion a dynamic of competition between the regions to obtain financial and legal resources from the central government. Regions sought to catch up with or stay ahead of the others. Competitive bargaining has been encouraged by the absence of co-decision making at the central level and of institutions of territorial cooperation such as an upper house on the "territorial chamber" model. Horizontal institutional collaboration among the Autonomous Communities (ACs) is virtually non-existent and intergovernmental relations between the central and the regional governments, particularly the Basque and the Catalan governments, are almost exclusively bilateral and vertical. In addition, the Constitutional Court has played a key role in the determination of responsibilities between levels of government.

Inter-party elite consensus among the two main state-wide parties, the Social Democratic PSOE and the right-wing PP, predominated in the development of the decentralization process. Nonetheless, the consensus faded at the end of 1990s and territorial cleavages have asserted themselves in the electoral process, notably provoked by the conservative party. Both parties use the presence of the regions they govern in federal and inter-regional institutions as a means to enhance party strategies. This is clearly the case of the recently created First Ministers' Conference, which also includes the prime minister and whose decisions must be consensually reached. Although it should meet annually, political polarization has reduced its frequency (only four conferences have been held since 2004) and party executives have clearly set the tone and the positions to be adopted. Because of the high level of vertical integration in political parties, the regional leaders have accepted these positions. The lack of a territorial chamber reinforces the importance of the extra-parliamentary party bodies.

The centre-periphery cleavage arises out of in the heterogeneous composition of Spanish society — in terms of ethnicity, language and culture. Public opinion surveys in the Basque Country and Catalonia show high levels of Catalan or Basque national identity, which is also present in Galician society, although, to a lesser extent. Decentralization has also generated a sense of common regional identity in other ACs where it did not previously exist or where it had been very weak.

Ethnic, linguistic and cultural cleavages are mirrored in the party system. Although, in the federal lower house, the effective number of parliamentary parties is small (2.5) because the two main country-wide parties have the vast proportion of seats, strong non country-wide Parties (NSWPs), nationalist or regionalist, have developed in several ACs, and regional parliaments typically contain the two main country-wide parties alongside one or more NSWPs. This has encouraged the national or country-wide parties to regionalize their electoral strategies, adjusting their manifestos to regional considerations and occasionally seeking coalitions with NSWPs.

The adoption of a regionalist face by national or country-wide parties, whose regional structures match the territorial design of the country, has been coupled with a high degree of vertical integration in the party structures together with limited autonomy for regional party branches.

On the one hand, national party statutes lay out how regional party branches must be structured while regional statutes must be approved by national executive bodies. Although the regional branches are formally in charge of party activities and finances at the AC level of government, in cases of open conflict between party levels, the national prevails.

On the other hand, regional leaders play a minor role in the selection of national federal leaders, but the federal party monitors who is elected at the regional level and intervenes (albeit informally) in the selection process, with a view to assuring that those elected belong to the same factions as the national leaders. Furthermore, candidates for the presidency of regional governments and assemblies must receive the formal approval of the central level, which also predominates in cases of conflicts over policies and coalition strategies.

As for civil society, most social organizations stick to local and regional boundaries. Civil society's distribution by levels of government is the following: 17 per cent federal, 37 per cent regional and 47 per cent local. Yet, the organization of civil society in Spain is guided by a territorial logic similar to that of the quasi-federal political structure of the country. Local organizations gather into regional networks or federations that simultaneously form state-wide coordination committees or confederations.

Both unions and the employers' associations are composed of a number of regional and sectoral federations, the former following the territorial political-administrative structure of Spain. The members of the regional federations are cross-sectoral provincial and local associations. Whereas non-economic country-wide associations, which are branches of international organizations, have centralized structures, national ones are usually products of bottom-up processes, in which local associations have federated and created central organs. The local level is responsible for daily activities, and the federal level takes care of common press releases, offers technical, logistical and legal advice, provides training to the affiliated organizations and represents them before national institutions in order to influence policy-making.

Territorial demands drive the organization of civil society in those regions that have strong and distinct identities. These regions, particularly Catalonia and the Basque Country, have seen the emergence of organizations which demand the recognition of their right to self-determination — a right not included in the Spanish Constitution.

Nowadays there is no consensus on territorial issues among the political parties. Controversial demands about the "nation", the distribution of powers, the financial system of the ACs, and the concept of inter-territorial solidarity and equal rights have entered into the Spanish political debate.

On one side, there are demands for greater decentralization and the recognition of a multinational Spain, coming mainly from Basque and Catalan nationalists and which the PSOE would be inclined to accept.

On the other side, there are demands for "re-centralization", on the basis of the unity of the Spanish nation and arguments based on rational political organization and efficiency in decision-making, mainly advanced by the PP. The territorial organization of the country and the building of an integrated political community are still contentious issues in Spain.

# The Swiss party system: Party federalism and no language-based party organizations

## ANDREAS LADNER / THOMAS MINGER

Swiss parties are politically far from homogenous. The cantonal parties play an important role and do not allow for a dominant party leadership at the national level, which weakens the influence of political parties. The federal structure of the party system, however, has been rather successful in preventing conflicts across denominational and linguistic borders. As well, the personalized and media-focused nature of politics make the cantonal parties significantly dependent on their national party organization. Their success in cantonal elections goes hand in hand with the performance of their national party.

On November 11, 2004 Swiss citizens took part in a popular vote on the reform of Swiss federalism. Prior to the vote, about one out of three cantonal party sections of the Social Democratic Party (SPS/PSS) and every fourth section of the Swiss People's Party did not follow their national party organization. The dissenting party sections of the Swiss People's Party (SVP/UDC) lost the vote while their national party organization was among the winners. At the same time, the dissenting sections of the Social Democrats won while their national party lost. The reform was broadly supported by the citizens. It resulted in a comfortable "yes" majority of 64.4 per cent and opened the way for a more modern and vibrant federalism.

Openly expressed dissent within parties is by no means exceptional in Switzerland and has not necessarily been considered as a fundamental weakness. It is much more the product of a "federalist" party system that leaves considerable leeway to party organizations at lower levels. Sometimes, it is even seen as an asset. On some issues, and especially when regional interests are concerned, divergent opinions cannot be ignored. Party federalism prevents single parties from undertaking arduous fights to achieve common positions. It even offers their voters a broader choice. They can support the line of the national party or that of the dissenting cantonal party sections.

The Swiss party system and, to a lesser extent, the system of civil society organizations closely follows the territorial fragmentation of the country. A cantonal party consists of its local party organizations which in general also organize and administer party membership. The national party consists of its cantonal party organizations. The bigger parties dispose of cantonal party organizations in almost every canton.

In Switzerland there are — and this has been very beneficial for internal peace and stability — no language based party organizations, as there are, for example in Belgium. All major parties include party organizations from the German, French and Italian speaking parts of the country. The parties must accommodate culturally divergent points of view internally. This has the effect of shielding national politics from quarrels among language groups.

Very much like the 26 cantons in the Swiss political system, it is the cantonal party organizations that form the core of the parties, especially among the less centralized center and right of center parties, as well as among the Greens. The cantonal parties all together dispose of much greater financial resources than the national party organizations and they employ a larger portion of party staff. This privileged position of the cantonal sections is supported by the fact that there are — as in parliamentary systems with different electoral constituencies — no nationwide elections, since the voting districts are the cantons. Neither is there a direct election of the government, nor an indirect election of a president or a prime minister, as for example in Germany, where the parties have an official candidate for the office of the "Bundeskanzler" (Chancellor). The important consequence of this predominance of the cantonal level is weak national party organizations and a lack of national leadership. The role of leader of a national party has to conciliate and manage a variety of political tendencies. Leaders are not elected for their political/ideological programs.

Since the constituent units of the federation enjoy a considerable amount of discretion in terms of public policies and tax rising powers, the cantonal party sections are at the heart of important political decisions. As well, reflecting the heterogeneity of the county which leads to considerable differences between cantons there are also considerable ideological differences among the cantonal sections of any single party.

The cantonal sections of the Social Democrats in the French speaking part of the country, for example, still have a more traditional, trade union orientation; whereas, in the German speaking part, they are more "modern", alternative or "New Labour" oriented. Similarly, the cantonal party sections of the Swiss liberal party (FDP.Die Liberalen/PLR.Les Libéraux-Radicaux), are more state oriented in the French speaking areas; whereas their counterparts in the German speaking part are more favourable to economic liberalization.

The national party organizations thus face an enormous amount of coordination work and often have difficulties in keeping all cantonal parties on a common track. Potential conflicts are alleviated by the Swiss federal principles of independence and separation of responsibilities. In 2003, when the Swiss People's Party wanted to expel Ms Widmer-Schlumpf, the national party had to expel the whole cantonal party section of Graubünden, where Widmer-Schlumpf was from.

However, there are also some more general factors that increase the pressure on the federal organization of the parties. The ongoing polarization of the Swiss party system, together with the media-focus and personalization of politics, calls for leadership and clear cut party positions. A national party leader has no time to consult the different cantonal parties when he has to defend the party line in a debate on TV; nor, on the other hand, can he make political statements that are not supported by cantonal parties.

Finally, the success of the cantonal parties even in cantonal elections depends more and more on the performance of the national parties. As a result of these new contingencies, it is inevitable that Switzerland will debate the idea of having more centralized party organizations.

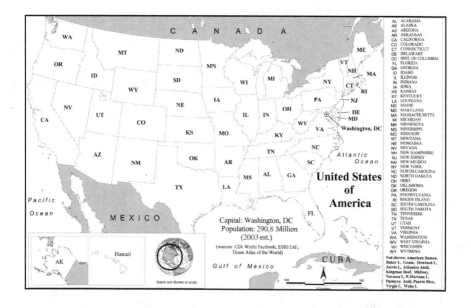

AL ALABAMA
AK ALASKA
AZ ARIZONA
AR ARKANSAS
CA CALIFORNIA
CO COLORADO
CT CONNECTICUT
DE DELAWARE
DC DIST. OF COLUMBIA
FL FLORIDA
GA GEORGIA
ID IDAHO
IL ILLINOIS
IN INDIANA
IA IOWA
KS KANSAS
KY KENTUCKY
LA LOUISIANA
ME MAINE
MD MARYLAND
MA MASSACHUSETTS
MI MICHIGAN
MN MINNESOTA
MS MISSISSIPPI
MO MISSOURI
MT MONTANA
NE NEBRASKA
NV NEVADA
NH NEW HAMPSHIRE
NJ NEW JERSEY
NM NEW MEXICO
NY NEW YORK
NC NORTH CAROLINA
ND NORTH DAKOTA
OH OHIO
OK OKLAHOMA
OR OREGON
PA PENNSYLVANIA
RI RHODE ISLAND
SC SOUTH CAROLINA
SD SOUTH DAKOTA
TN TENNESSEE
TX TEXAS
UT UTAH
VT VERMONT
VA VIRGINIA
WA WASHINGTON
WV WEST VIRGINIA
WI WISCONSIN
WY WYOMING

Not shown: American Samoa,
Baker I., Guam, Howland I.,
Jarvis I., Johnston Atoll,
Kingman Reef, Midway,
Navassa I., N.Mariana I.,
Palmyra Atoll, Puerto Rico,
Virgin I., Wake I.

# Political Parties, Civil Society, and American Federalism.

## GARY WEKKIN / JOE HOWARD

The ups and downs of the American federal experience commend the United States not as a model for would-be federations to imitate, but as a primer of valuable lessons about federal practice. The greatest of these lessons is that federalism, although imperfect, can endure over time, despite its internal contradictions.

Federalism is a bargain — the promise of unity amidst diversity — in order to enjoy the benefits of each, without sacrificing either. The challenge is to keep competing centripetal and centrifugal forces in balance. The accelerating pace of change across time continuously stresses the federal bargain by requiring constant adjustments in order to maintain equilibrium. The polar alternatives of unitary government or of "disunion" can seem invitingly simple in comparison.

For this reason, the historic oscillation of American federalism between a state-centered compact and an indestructible union illustrates that a "federal culture" — i.e., the sensitivity of civil society to changes of equilibrium between shared community and separate identities — and a flexible and adaptable federal arrangement are as essential to federalism as such basic structural elements as the constitutional division of powers. Without muscles and nerves to direct them, a skeleton is a necessary, but not a sufficient, condition for life.

In American civil society, changes of societal equilibrium — such as wars, economic booms and recessions, waves of immigration, and innovations in technology — have been followed by eruptions of popular passions and interests. These fostered the formation of organized interest groups, which seek collective political expression of identity and want. It is the role of more than 8,000 such interest groups to articulate the social ferment that persistently interrupts the sociopolitical equilibrium. And it has been the role of two elite-cadre political parties that have endured since the 1800s (thanks to plurality, first-past-the-post elections) to aggregate such evolving diversity into politically manageable alternatives from which the voting millions may choose.

Republicans and Democrats are not unlike Coca Cola and Pepsi Cola — similar products that differ more in iconography and association than in formula and effect.

However, democratic choice is served insofar as both parties would rather govern than not, and have a will to compete with each other in order to do so. It is in this relentless competition for electoral favour, rather than in divergent programs, that the two major American political parties serve democracy.

This is not to say that policy does not matter in American politics, but rather that competition for the median voter forces both parties to position themselves programmatically nearer the political center of the electorate than to its polar margins. It is tempting to credit the political parties for the durability of American federalism. Their elasticity, their willingness to accommodate increasing diversity and longitudinal change in order to achieve and maintain winning coalitions has facilitated the continuity of the American state from a more limited, residual past to the constantly adapting inclusivity of the present. Each party serves as the public commons in which the claims of competing interest groups, foundations, nonprofits, and online communities within its electoral coalition are reconciled in order to compete with the opposing party for the right to direct public policy.

Both major political parties, and most interest groups, are organized along the unmistakable lines of American federal architecture. Since significant domestic governing powers, including the making of election laws, are reserved by the Tenth Amendment to the 50 American states, Democrats and Republicans are compelled to organize principally at the state level, and then quilt themselves together in order to compete for national power.

The sheer diversity of the states themselves, (compounded by the dissemination across them of a variety of nominating procedures and party regulations) effectively rendered the national Democratic and Republican party organizations as weak confederations until the 1970s. Since then, the national Democrats' adoption and enforcement of guidelines for state party selection of delegates to presidential nominating conventions, and the national

Republicans' pioneering adaptations of technology for fund-raising and voter contacting have engendered an upward flow of power in each party. We see this in the mixed success of certain state parties at advancing the dates of their presidential primaries in 2008. However, the "venue-shopping" of various 2008 presidential candidates, who invested their campaign resources in early state contests, or minimized their efforts in states in which certain minority voters would be key, or contested states with primaries open only to partisan identifiers, signifies the extent to which the federal maze of American states and communities remains a complex ecology that not only permits, but encourages, a diverse civil society to thrive.

Interest groups have incentive to venue-shop this complex ecology as well. Although every state wields similar domestic powers, not every state government has the same degree of institutional development or fiscal capacity, and not every state electorate shares the same expectations of state government. Where the capacities of state governments are lower, larger capitalized interests may roam freer of taxes and regulation, and nonprofits have more opportunity to spring up as entrepreneurial responses to national domestic initiatives. Where "low tax, low service" norms prevail, nonprofit service vendors may be actively encouraged by regional as well as national authorities. The 50 states and their numerous counties, municipalities, and local government districts function as a vast complex of laboratories for the research and development of service delivery as well as of policy content, and as economic stimulus packages for suppliers of private goods, as well.

American civil society is not limited to parties and interest groups. Numerous nongovernmental organizations, ranging from foundation think tanks to nonprofit service providers to online communities, have assumed increasingly prominent roles in electoral and policy debate. Online technology has enabled users sharing values to network across distance, revolutionizing the building and deployment of social capital by permitting influence to flow horizontally, rather than hierarchically. Online fundraising and voter mobilization and outreach to niche blogging communities were prominent in the 2004 and 2008 election campaigns. They raised the ceiling for future distance-networking strategies as wireless technology spreads. However, the democratization of discourse enabled by such technology also facilitates negative campaigning. The 2008 campaign occasioned much viral spreading of false claims and manipulated images, some of which were re-circulated by traditional news media that Americans still trust to broker voting information.

Federalism creates a complex ecology that encourages many political species to survive and develop in their niches. But to have voice very far beyond one's niche also requires coalescence with others when and where possible. The logic of collective action is an inescapable reality in any mass society, federal or not. Thus, the effect of systemic interaction between federal structure and civil society must be taken into account in order to understand most aspects of American politics.

# Glossary

ASYMMETRIC FEDERALISM.    Unequal or non-identical distribution of powers and responsibilities between the constituent units of a federal system; e.g. the greater autonomy accorded the Basque Country, Catalonia and Navarre than the other AUTONOMOUS COMMUNITIES in Spain.

AUTONOMOUS COMMUNITIES.    The 17 territorial units of the Spanish state; created under the 1978 democratic constitution but not technically constituent units since their role and status has evolved through a process of devolution or FEDERALIZATION.

BROKERAGE PARTIES.    Canadian term for a political party that brings together and represents a broad range of sometimes divergent interest and social groups.

*BUNDESKANZLER* (federal chancellor).    Head of Government of the German federation.

*BUNDESRAT* (federal council).    Second chamber of the German federal parliament, representing the *LÄNDER*.

CANTONS.    Name of the 26 constituent units of the Swiss federation.

CIVIL SOCIETY.    The range of organizations and networks that individuals form distinct from government or business.

CLASS-BASED PARTY.    A political party whose primary — though not exclusive — appeal is to voters as members of an economic class; essentially the labour or social-democratic parties.

COMPULSORY VOTING.    Laws prevailing across Australia stipulating, as the *Commonwealth Electoral Act 1918* puts it, that 'It shall be the duty of every elector to vote at each election' and imposing a penalty for non-compliance.

CONFEDERALISM.    Decentralised form of union where sovereignty and most powers reside with the CONSTITUENT UNITS and the central government has little direct relationship with the people.

CONGRESS.    Name of major political party in India (Indian National Congress); also Nigeria and South Africa (ANC). Name of national legislature in Mexico and USA.

CONSOCIATIONALISM.    Practice of representing major linguistic or religious communities in democratic processes through peak organisational structures ('pillars').

CONSTITUENT UNITS.   The jurisdictions into which a federation is divided, enjoying constitutional status as partners in the union — called STATES, PROVINCES, *LÄNDER,* CANTONS or REGIONS depending on the particular federation.

CORPORATISM.   Highly structured representation of main economic interest groups with peak organizations negotiating outcomes between themselves and with government (not to be confused with CONSOCIATIONALISM, which involves culturally- rather than economically-defined groups).

CULTURAL COMMUNITIES.   The non-geographic CONSTITUENT UNITS of the Belgian federation.

DUAL FEDERALISM.   Traditional model in the Anglo federations where the two orders of government operate to large extent in their own separate spheres of jurisdiction.

FEDERALIZATION.   Process of moving incrementally toward federalism by constitutional devolution of authority

FIRST-PAST-THE-POST (FPTP) ELECTORAL SYSTEM.   Informal term for *single-member plurality* electoral systems where the candidate with the most votes is declared the winner in each electoral district regardless of whether they received a majority votes or not; favours TWO-PART SYSTEM.

HISTORICAL REGIONS.   The AUTONOMOUS COMMUNITIES in Spain that have enjoyed a privileged access to autonomous status because of their distinct cultural and historical identities.

INTERLOCKED FEDERAL SYSTEM.   The German model of federalism where authority is not divided between the national government and the *LÄNDER* so much on the basis of policy domains as between an overarching responsibility for policy frameworks and a *LÄNDER* responsibility for implementation and administration, with the *LÄNDER* enjoying a high degree of representation in national policy-making through the *BUNDESRAT.*

LAND.   Singular of *Länder.*

LÄNDER.   Name for the CONSTITUENT UNITS of the German and Austrian federations; equivalent to States or provinces (singular: *LAND*).

MINOR PARTY.   Political parties too small to form government on their own or as senior members of a coalition and which may be disadvantaged under the FIRST-PAST-THE-POST (FPTP) ELECTORAL SYSTEM; also known as 'third parties' for their peripheral status in two-party systems.

MUNICIPALITIES.   Third tier of government in a federation, not enjoying constitutional status on a par with the national government or the constituent units.

PLEBISCITARY DEMOCRACY.   Democracy where government makes regular use of referendums to advance its agenda.

PROTECTIONISTS.   Parliamentarians in the early years after Federation in Australia who advocated a program of tariff protectionism for manufacturing industry.

PROVINCES.   Term for the CONSTITUENT UNITS of the federation in Argentina, Canada and South Africa.

STATE OF AUTONOMIES.   Direct translation of the formal term for the quasi-federal Spanish constitutional order.

STATES.   Name for the constituent units in the federations of Australia (6 States), Brazil (26 States), India (28 States), Mexico (31 States), Nigeria (36 States), United States of America (50 States).

SWING VOTERS.   Voters who are not regular supporters of one particular party but 'swing' towards the party they find most appealing in any given election.

TWO-PARTY SYSTEM.   A party system where two major parties regularly receive, between them, the great majority of votes and between whom the political process tends to be polarized.

UNION GOVERNMENT.   Term for the central government in India.

VENUE SHOPPING.   Tendency of some interest groups to advance their cause at the level or location of government where they can achieve the most success — taking advantage of the multiplicity of governments in a federal system.

# Contributors

NORMAN ABJORENSEN, Research Director at the Parliamentary Studies Centre, Crawford School of Economics and Government, The Australian National University, Canberra, Australia.

OKON AKIBA, Professor of Comparative and International Relations at Clark Atlanta University, USA.

JAVIER ASTUDILLO, Lecturer in the Department of Political and Social Sciences of the Universitat Pompeu Fabra, Barcelona, Spain; and Adjunct Faculty Member of the Department of Political Science at the University of North Carolina at Chapel Hill, United States of America.

WILLIAM CROSS, Professor and Bell Chair in Canadian Parliamentary Democracy in the Department of Political Science at Carleton University, Ottawa, Canada.

KLAUS DETTERBECK, Assistant Professor at the Institute of Political Science, University of Magdeburg, Magdeburg, Germany.

JOE HOWARD, Assistant Professor of Political Science at the University of Central Arkansas in Conway, Arkansas, United States of America.

JEAN-FRANÇOIS PRUD'HOMME, Professor and General Academic Coordination at El Colegio de Mexico, Mexico City, Mexico.

JIBRIN IBRAHIM, Director of the Center for Democracy and Development, Abuja, Nigeria.

ANDREAS LADNER, Professor Swiss administration and political institutions at the Swiss Graduate School of Public Administration (IDHEAP), Lausanne, Switzerland.

THOMAS MINGER, Conference of the Cantonal Governments, Switzerland.

FRANCESC PALLARES, Professor of Political Science at the Universitat Pompeu Fabra, Barcelona, Spain.

WOLFGANG RENZSCH J., Professor of Political Science and Jean-Monnet-Chair for European Studies at Magdeburg University, Magdeburg, Germany.

SANDEEP SHASTRI, Director of the International Academy for Creative Teaching at Bangalore, India.

CHRIS TAPSCOTT, Professor and Dean of the Faculty of Economic and Management Sciences at the University of the Western Cape, Cape Town, South Africa.

FRANCIS KOK WAH LOH, Professor of Politics in the School of Social Sciences, Universiti Sains Malaysia, Penang, Malaysia.

GARY WEKKIN, Professor of Political Science at the University of Central Arkansas in Conway, Arkansas, United States of America.

LIEVEN DE WINTER, Professor at the Université Catholique de Louvain (where he is co-director of the *Pôle Interuniversitaire sur l'Opinion publique et la Politique*, PIOP), Belgium.

CAROLINE VAN WYNESBERGHE, Researcher at the UCL's Centre de science politique et de politique comparée and a lecturer at the Catholic university of Mons (FUCaM), Belgium.

# Participating Experts

We gratefully acknowledge the input of the following experts who participated in the theme of Political Parties and Civil Society in Federal Countries. While participants contributed their knowledge and experience, they are in no way responsible for the contents of this booklet.

Hussaini Abdu, Country Director, Action Aid Nigeria, Nigeria

Ahmad Fauzi Abdul Hamid, Associate Professor, Universiti Sains, Malaysia

Hamdan Abdul Majeed, Senior Vice President, Khazanah Research and Investment Strategy, Malaysia

Solomon Abgu, Lecturer, Department of Political Science, University of Abuja, Nigeria

Norman Abjorensen, Visiting Fellow in the School of Social Sciences, Policy and Governance Program, Crawford School of Economics and Government, Australian National University, Australia

Yasmeen Abu-Laban, Professor, Department of Political Science, University of Alberta, Canada

Amanda Acedo, Deputy at the Navarre Parliament, Socialist Party of Navarre, Spain

Tunde Agara, Lecturer, Igbinedion University, Okada, Nigeria

Miguel J. Agudo, Senior Lecturer Constitutional Law, Universidad de Córdoba, Spain

Oduenyi Ahanekum, Technical Adviser, Constitutional Reform Dialogue Mechanism, Nigeria

Eliseo Aja, President, Council of Statutary Guarantees of Catalonia, Spain

WumiAjibiaro Dada, Senior Project Manager, WRAPA/GAA, Nigeria

Okon Akiba, Professor, Department of Comparative and International Relations, University of Clark Atlanta, Nigeria

Taiwo Akinwande, Administrative Officer, Centre for Democracy and Development, Nigeria

Carlos Alba, Professor, El Colegio de México, Mexico

Ahmadu Aliyu, Executive Assistant to the Director, Centre for Democracy and Development, Nigeria

Rufai Alkali, Publicity Secretary, People's Democratic Party, Abuja, Nigeria
Hussain Alyami, President of Saudi Arab Club, University of Central Arkansas, United States of America.
Hans Ambühl, Generalsekretär, Schweizerische Konferenz der kantonalen Erziehungsdirektoren, Switzerland
Lawal Amodu, Programme officer, Constitutional Reform Dialogue Mechanism, Nigeria
Mustafa Kamal Anuar, Lecturer, Universiti Sains, Malaysia
Joshua Anyacho, Citizens Forum for Constitutional Reform, Nigeria
Clay Arnold, Professor and Chair, Political Science Department, University of Central Arkansas, United States of America.
Balveer Arora, Professor, Jawaharlal Nehru University, India
Javier Astudillo, Lecturer Political Science, Universitat Pompeu Fabra, Spain
Ikowo Attah, Reporter, DBN TV, Nigeria
Alberto Aziz, Professor, Centro de Investigaciones y Estudios Superiores en Antropología Social, México
Kenny Bafo, Post Graduate student, The University of the Western Cape, South Africa
Chom Bagu, Adviser, USAID, Nigeria
Mallam Bappa Salihu, Ahmadu Bello University, Zaria, Nigeria
Silvia Bär, stv. Generalsekretärin, SVP Schweiz, Switzerland
Juan A. Barrio, Deputy at the Spanish Congress Socialist Workers Party, Spain
Pierre Baudewyns, Researcher, Université catholique de Louvain, Belgium
Ralf Thomas Baus Leiter, Team Innenpolitik, Hauptabteilung Politik und Beratung, Konrad-Adenauer-Stiftung, Germany
Rodolfo Benito, Director, Fundación 1º de Mayo — Comisiones Obreras, Spain
Sabine Bergstermann, Team Innenpolitik, Hauptabteilung Politik und Beratung, Konrad-Adenauer-Stiftung, Germany
Dwaipayan Bhattacharya, Fellow, Centre for Studies in Social Sciences, Calcutta, India
Ilán Bizberg, Professor, El Colegio de México, Mexico
Thierry Bodson, Secrétaire general, FGTB wallonne, Belgium
Lorenz Bösch Regierungsrat, Präsident, CVP SZ, KdK, Switzerland
Julia von Blumenthal, Professor, Humboldt-Universität zu Berlin, Institut für Sozialwissenschaften Germany
Guillermo Cejudo, Professor, Centro de Investigación y Docencia Económicas, Mexico
Rupak Chattopadhyay, Vice President, Forum of Federations, India
David Chernushenko, President, Green & Gold Inc., Canada
Ahmad Chik, Penang Heritage Trust, Malaysia
Yee Whah Chin, Associate Professor, Universiti Sains, Malaysia
Kong Yeow Chow, National Vice-Chairman Democratic Action Party, Malaysia
Rekha Chowdhary, Professor, University of Jammu, India
Ann Clemmer, State Representative, Arkansas House of Representatives, United States of America.
Claus-Peter Clostermeyer, Head of the Department of Political Affairs in Berlin, Vertretung des Landes, Baden-Württemberg beim Bund, Germany.

Timothy Conlan, Professor, Government and Politics, George Mason University, United States of America

James Connor, Lecturer, University of New South Wales - School of Australian Defence Force Academy, Australia

Brian Costar, Professor, Faculty of Life and Social Sciences, Swinburne University, Australia

William Cross, Professor and Bell Chair in Canadian Parliamentary Democracy in the Department of Political Science at Carleton University, Ottawa, Canada

Régis Dandoy, Researcher, Université Libre de Bruxelles, Belgium

Daniel Furter, Parteisekretär, SP BE, Switzerland

Lieven De Winter, Professor, Université catholique de Louvain, Belgium

Kris Deschouwer Hoogleraar, Vrije Universiteit Brussel, Belgium

Rajeshwari Deshpande, Professor, University of Pune, India

Klaus Detterbeck, Senior Researcher and Lecturer, Otto-v.-Guericke-Univ. Magdeburg, Institut für Politikwissenschaft, Germany

Veena Devi, Reader, Department of Political Science, Bangalore University, Bengaluru, India

Carl Devos Docent, Universiteit Gent, Belgium

Hans-Jörg Dietsche, Referent für Rechtspolitik, Geschäftsführer des Bundesarbeitskreises, Christian Democratic Union of Germany, Germany

Price Dooley, Lecturer,University of Central Arkansas, United States of America.

Steve Dovers, Lecturer, Australian National University, Australia

Roslyn Dundas, Director, ACT Council of Social Service Inc., Australia

Victor Egwemi, Secretary, Nigerian Political Science Association, Nigeria

Sam Egwu, Head of Governance Unit, United Nations Development Programme, Nigeria

Daniel Ehighalua, Secretary, Nigeria Coalition on the International Criminal Court, Nigeria

Chinedu Elekwachi, Reporter, New Nigeria Newspaper, Nigeria

Paul Elton, Deputy Head of Secretariat, Council of Australian Governments Reform Council, Australia

Chong Eng, Member of Parliament, Democratic Action Party, Malaysia

Azeem Farouk, Lecturer, Universiti Sains, Malaysia

Doris Fischer-Taeschler, Parteipräsidentin, FDP.Die Liberalen AG, Switzerland

André Flahaut, Vice-Président, Chambre des Représentants, Parti Socialiste, Belgium

Laura Flamand, Professor, El Colegio de México, Mexico

Tully Fletcher, Student / Research Assistant, Australian National University, Australia

Marius Fransman, MP National Assembly, African National Council, South Africa

Ralph Freese, CEO, Spier Leasure Holdings, South Africa

Pascal Furer, Parteisekretär, SVP AG, Switzerland

Aliyu Garba, Research Officer, Institute of Governance and Social Research, Nigeria

Sven Gatz, Fractievoorzitter Open VLD, Vlaams Parlement, Belgium

Rajeev Gowda, Professor and Congress leader, Indian Institute of Management, Bangalore, India

Mireia Grau, Responsible of Research, Institut d'Estudis Autonòmics, Spain

Virginia Gray, Distinguish.Professor, Political Science Department, University of North Carolina, United States

Tonatiuh Guillén, Director, El Colegio de la Frontera, Norte, Mexico

Janet Harris, Deputy Secretary of State, State of Arkansas, United States

Melissa Haussman, Professor, Department of Political Science, Carleton University, Canada

Terfa Hemen, Assistant Program Officer, Centre for Democracy and Development, Nigeria

Reinold Herber, Senior Advisor, Forum of Federations, Germany

Rogelio Hernández, Professor, El Colegio de México, Mexico

Hans Hofmann, Team Leader, Federal Chancellery of Germany, Germany

Rainer Holtschneider, former State Secretary of Saxony-Anhalt, Germany

Joseph Howard, Assistant Professor, Political Science, University of Central Arkansas, United States

Paul Huber, ehemaliger Regierungsrat, SP LU, Switzerland

Jibrin Ibrahim, Director, Centre for Democracy and Development, Nigeria

Udo Jude Ilo, Program Manager, Forum of Federations, Nigeria

Ernesto Isunza, Professor, Centro de Investigaciones y Estudios Superiores en Antropología Social, Jalapa, Mexico

James Jacob, Lecturer, Department of Political Science, University of Abuja, Nigeria

Chenraj Jain, Chancellor, Jain University, India

Jan Fivaz, Gründungsmitglied/Wisenschaftlicher Mitarbeiter, smartvote, Switzerland

Abbas Jimoh, Reporter, Daily Trust Newpaper, Nigeria

Víctor Juan, Professor, el Instituto de Investigaciones Sociológicas de la Universidad Autónoma Benito Juárez de Oaxaca, Mexico

Uwe Jun, Professor, Abteilung der Politikwissenschaft, Universität Trier, Germany

Radha Krishna K.E, Political Activist, JDS-Janata Dal (S), India

Khay Jin Khoo, Malaysia

Brad Kinsela, Queensland Government, Australia

Felix Knüpling, Director, Europe Programs, Forum of Federations, Germany

Royce Koop, Post-Doctoral Fellow, Dept of Political Science, Memorial University of Newfoundland, Canada

Regine Kramer, Policy Coordinator Institutional Affairs, Assembly of European Regions, Belgium

Uwe Kranenpohl, Professor, Politik und Verwaltungswissenschaften, Evangelische Fachhochshule Nürnberg, Germany

Hendrik C. Krauskopf, Wissenschaftlicher Mitarbeiter, Institut de hautes études en administration publique, Switzerland

Veeriah Krishnasamy, Secretary, Malaysian Trade Union Congress, Penang Division, Malaysia

Volker Kröning, Senator a.D., Senate of Bremen, Germany

Jeevan Kumar, Professor of Political Science, Bangalore University, India

Sanjay Kumar, Fellow, Centre for the Study of Developing Societies, India
Gopa Kumar, Professor and Head, Department of Political Science, University of Kerala, India
Sujith Kumar, Assistant Professor, Political Science Department, University of Central Arkansas, United States
Chris Kwaja, Lecturer, Centre for Conflict Management and Peace Studies, University of Jos, Nigeria
Andreas Ladner, Institut de hautes études en administration publique, Switzerland
Bernadette Lambrechts, Ancienne chef de Cabinet, Cabinet Vice-premier Ministre Milquet, Cabinet Ministre Fonck, Belgium
Phil Larkin, Senior Lecturer, Faculty of Business & Government, University of Canberra, Australia
Ching-Tong Liew, Member of Parliament, Democratic Action Party, Malaysia
Kah Cheng Lim, Lawyer, Malaysia
Sanjay Lodha, Professor, MLS University, Udaipur, India
John Lofton, Assistant Professor, Arkansas State University, United States
Robert Lowry, Professor, University of Texas, Dallas, United States
Georg Lutz, Projektleiter Wahlforschung, Swiss Foundation for Research in Social Sciences, Switzerland
Sandra Maissen, Geschäftsleitende Sekretärin, Konferenz der Kantonsregierungen, Switzerland
Jonathan Malloy, Professor, Department of Political Science, Carleton University, Canada
Ian Marsh, Lecturer, University of Tasmania, Australian Innovation Research Centre, Australia
Nick Martin, Australian Labor Party, Australia
Louis Massicotte, Professor, Department of Political Science, Université de Laval, Canada
Kabir Mato, Lecturer, University of Abuja, Department of Political Science, Nigeria
Bob Mattes, Director Democracy in Africa Research Unit, Department of Politics, University of Cape Town, South Africa
Tom McInnis, Professor, Political Science Department, University of Central Arkansas, United States
Sabelo Mczinziba, ANC Youth League, the University of the Western Cape, South Africa
Ajay Mehra, Director (Honorary), Centre for Public Affairs, India
Thomas Minger, Leiter Bereich Innenpolitik, Konferenz der Kantonsregierungen, Switzerland
Philippe Monfils, Sénateur, Ministre d'Etat, Sénat, Belgium
Tobias Montag, Team Innenpolitik, Hauptabteilung Politik und Beratung, Konrad-Adenauer-Stiftung, Germany
Carlos Moreno, Professor, Universidad Jesuita de Guadalajara, Mexico
Mark Mullenbach, Associate Professor, Political Science Department, University of Central Arkansas, United States

David Müller, Geschäftsführer, FDP.Die Liberalen, Switzerland
Sreekanta Murthy, Congress Party, India
Auwal Musa Rafsanjani, Executive Director, Civil Society Legislative Advocacy
Centre, Nigeria
Jayaprakash Narayan, President, Lok Satta Party, India
Barry Naughten, The Australian National University, Australia
Daniel Nengak, Program Officer, Nigeria Gender Budget Network, Nigeria
Anil Netto Aliran, Treasurer, ALIRAN, Malaysia
Viola Neu, Koordinatorin Wahl- und Parteienforschung, Team Innenpolitik,
Hauptabteilung Politik und Beratung, Konrad-Adenauer-Stiftung, Germany
Cecilia Ng, Visiting Professor, Universiti Sains, Malaysia
Ik Tien Ngu, Post Graduate, Universiti Sains, Malaysia
Clement Nwankwo, Lawyer and Executive Director, Policy Legal Advocacy Centre,
Nigeria
Rob Oakeshott, Member of Parliament (MP), Australian House of Representatives,
Australia
Peter Ocheikwu, Program Officer, Open Society Initiative for West Africa, Nigeria
Jide Ojo, Senior Program Officer, United Nations Development Programme,
Nigeria
Eyene Okpanachi, Doctoral Candidate, Department of Political Science, University of Ibadan, Nigeria
Alberto Olvera, Professor, Universidad Veracruzana, Mexico
Reynaldo Ortega, Professor, El Colegio de México, Mexico
Ramakrishan P, President, ALIRAN, Malaysia
Dharma P.L. Dr.Professor, Mangalore University, India
B.S Padmavathi, Sr.Fellow, Jain University, India
Martin  Papillon, Professor, University of Ottawa, Canada
Kevin Patrick, Development Consultant, Independent, South Africa
Nancy Peckford, Executive Director, Equal Voice: Electing More Women in Canada,
Canada
Jean-Benoît Pilet, Professeur, Université Libre de Bruxelles, Belgium
Laurence Piper, Head of Department, Department of Political Studies, the University of the Western Cape, South Africa
Eva Pleguezuelos, Member, Themis. Association of Women Lawyers, Spain
Chandrashekar Prabhu, Editor Economic Digest, India
Isabelle Praile, Vice-Présidente, Exécutif des Musulmans de Belgique, Belgium
Scott Prasser, Professor and Executive Director, Public Policy Institute, Australian
Cathoilic University, Public Policy Institute Australia
Jean François Prud'homme, VP Academic, El Colegio de México, Mexico
Garrett  Purtill, Australian Capital Territory, Legislative Assembly, Australia
Demetri Qually, Councillor — South Peninsula sub council, Democratic Alliance,
South Africa
E.Raghavan, Former Editor, South Economic Times India, Center for Excellence
in Social Sciences and Education, India

Harish Ramaswamy, Professor, Karnataka University, India
Volker Ratzmann, Fraktionsvorsitzender, Green Parliamentary Group in the Abgeordnetenhaus, Germany
David Recondo, Professor, Sciences Po Paris, France
Ramasanjeeva Reddy, Advocate & Tax Consultant, Congress Party, India
Gabriele Reitmeier, Regionalreferat Mittelmeerländer/Afrika, Politikberatung und Int. Politikanalyse, Friedrich-Naumann-Stiftung für die Freiheit, Germany
Wolfgang Renzsch, Jean-Monnet Chair of European Studies, Otto-v.-Guericke-Univ. Magdeburg, Institut für Politikwissenschaft, Germany
Horst Risse, Abteilungsleiter, Information u. Dokumentation, Deutscher Bundestag, Germany
David Robertson, Curator's Teaching Professor, Political Science Department, University of Missouri, United States of America
Raimund Rodewald, Geschäftsleiter Stiftung Landschaftsschutz Schweiz, Switzerland
Sandra Rosvelds, Diensthoofd Studiedienst, ACW, Belgium
Bill (William) Rowlings, Secretary, Civil Liberties Australia, Australia
Abubakar Saddique Mohammed, Lecturer, Ahmadu Bello University, Zaria, Nigeria
Tunde Salman, People and Passion Consult Ltd., Nigeria
Will Sanders, Lecturer, Australian National University, Australia
Marian Sawer, Professor, School of Social Sciences, College of Arts and Social Sciences, Australian National University, Australia
Margreth Schär, Fraktionspräsidentin des Grossen Rates, SP BE, Switzerland
Florian Schartau, Koordinator Kommunalpolitik, Team Innenpolitik, Hauptabteilung Politik und Beratung, Konrad-Adenauer-Stiftung, Germany
Matthias Schenker, Ressortleiter Politik, Santésuisses, Switzerland
Wolfgang Schröder, Professor, Universität Kassel, Germany
Martin Schwegler, Parteipräsident, CVP LU, Switzerland
Leslie Seidle, Senior Policy Advisor, Forum of Federations, Canada
Chris Serroyen, Hoofd Studiedienst, ACV-CSC, Belgium
Zed Seselja, Liberal Party of Australia, Australia
Chrissy Sharp, Small Tree Farm, Australia
Sandeep Shastri, Pro-Vice Chancellor, Jain University, India
Otto Sieber, Zentralsekretär, Pro Natura - Schweizerischer Bund für Naturschutz, Switzerland
Dave Sinardet, Postdoctoraal onderzoeker FWO/ Deeltijds Professor, Universiteit Antwerpen, Facultés Universitaires Saint-Louis & Vrije Universiteit Brussel, Belgium
Fernanda Somuano, Professor, El Colegio de México, Mexico
Willibald Sonnleitner, Professor, El Colegio de México, Mexico
Jean-François, Steiert Nationalrat, SP FR, Switzerland
Ursula Stephens, Senator, Australian House of Representatives, Australia
Abubakar Sulaima, Lecturer, Department of Political Science, University of Abuja, Nigeria
David Sullivan, Senator, Australian House of Representatives, Australia
K.C Suri, Professor, University of Hyderabad, India

Joanna Sweet, Graduate Student, Carleton University, Canada
Wilfried Swenden, Senior Lecturer, University of Edinburgh, Belgium
Geo Taglioni, Leiter Politik und Partizipation national, Schweizerische Arbeitsgemeinschaft der Jugendverbände, Switzerland
Christopher Tapscott, Dean of the Faculty of Economic & Management Sciences, the University of the Western Cape, South Africa
Benny The, Lecturer, Universiti Sains, Malaysia
Lisa Thompson, Director, African Centre for Citizenship and Democracy, the University of the Western Cape, South Africa
Gizachew Tiruneh, Assistant Professor, Political Science Department, University of Central Arkansas, United States of America
Lechesa Tsenoldi, MP National Assembly, African National Council, South Africa
Dirk Van Melkebeke, Kabinetschef Kabinet, Vice-ministre president, Lieten, Belgium
Caroline Van Wynsberghe, Researcher, Université catholique de Louvain, Belgium
Kurt Vandaele, Researcher, European Trade Union Institute, Belgium
Hugo Vandenberghe, Eerste ondervoorzitter, Senaat, Belgium
Pierre Verjans, Chargé de cours, Université de Liège, Belgium
Emanuel Waeber-Vonlanthen, Parteipräsident CVP FR, Switzerland
Stefaan Walgrave, Universiteit Antwerpen, Belgium
Clement Wasah, Executive Director, Community Action for Popular Participation, Nigeria
David Wegede, Reporter, DBN TV, Nigeria
Roman Widmer, Assistenz Sekretär, Konferenz der Kantonsregierungen, Switzerland
John Wilkerson, Staff Attorney, Arkansas Municipal League, United States
John Williams, Professor, School of Government, the University of the Western Cape, South Africa
Bernard Wright, Clerk, Australian House of Representatives, Australia
Aliyu Yahaya, Lecturer, Ahmadu Bello University, Zaria, Nigeria
Jonathan Yeoh, Research Officer, Penang State Government, Malaysia
Leong Yueh Kwong, Executive Director, Socio-Economic Research Institute, Malaysia
Esther Yusuf, Constitutional Reform Dialogue Mechanism, Nigeria
Ruslan Zainuddin, Lecturer, Universiti Utara, Malaysia
Udo Zolleis, leader of the Bavarian legislature's planning staff, Bayerischer Landtag, Germany

## Diversity and Unity in Federal Countries
### Edited by César Colino and Luis Moreno
### Senior Editor, John Kincaid

Published for the Forum of Federations and the International Association of Centers for Federal Studies (IACFS)
Global Dialogue on Federalism, Book Series, Volume 7

Examines the balance of diversity and unity in twelve federal or federal-type countries (Australia, Belgium, Brazil, Canada, Ethiopia, Germany, India, Nigeria, Russian, Spain, Switzerland and the United States of America). Leading scholars and practitioners illustrate the current political, socio-economic, spatial, and cultural diversity in their country before delving into the role that social, historical and political factors have had in shaping the present balance of diversity and unity. Authors assess the value that is placed on diversity by examining whether present institutional arrangements and public policies either restrict or enhance it, and address the future challenges of balancing diversity and unity in an increasingly populated and mobile world.

Authors include: Nicholas Aroney, Balveer Arora, Petra Bendel, Irina Busygina, César Colino, Frank Delmartino, Hugues Dumont, Marcus Faro de Castro, Assefa Fiseha, Thomas Fleiner, Alain-G. Gagnon, Mohammed Habib, Andreas Heinemann-Grüder, Maya Hertig Randall, John Kincaid, Gilberto Marcos Antonio Rodrigues, Luis Moreno, Richard Simeon, Roland Sturm, Rotimi T. Suberu, Sébastien Van Drooghenbroeck.

JOHN KINCAID is Professor of Government and Public Service and director of the Robert B. and Helen S. Meyner Center for the Study of State and Local Government at Lafayette College, Easton, Pennsylvania.
LUIS MORENO is a Research Professor at the Centre for Human and Social Sciences, Spanish National Research Council (CSIC), Spain.
CÉSAR COLINO is an Associate Professor at the Universidad Nacional de Educación a Distancia, Spain.

December 2008
6 x 9  12 maps

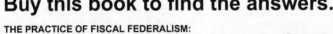

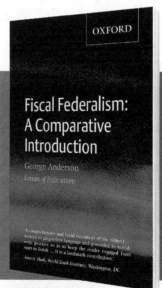

# A primer on federalism

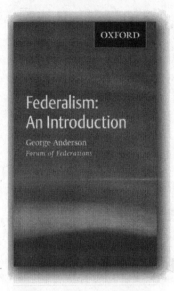

This admirably concise book, written by George Anderson, a leading expert on federalism and head of the Forum of Federations, provides a straightforward, jargon-free intro - duction to the topic. It is essential reading not only for students and those in government, but for ordinary citizens of the world's federations. (Available in English, Arabic, Kurdish and Nepali)

Inside this book are explanations of many of the mysteries of federal countries, including:

- How federal countries arose
- What makes a country federal
- How money is handled
- Diversity in federal countries
- How powers are divided

# Occasional Paper Series

Discussions on policy-oriented, sectoral issues in federal systems. Available in print or online.

**Occasional Paper Number 1:**
**Pension Reform in Canada: An Often Fractious Federation**
By Bruce Little
©2010 Forum of Federations, 20 pages, ISSN 1922-558X (print), CA$6

Available free online at www.forumfed.org

**Foreign Occasional Paper Number 2: Development Policy of Constituent Units: Trends, Challenges and Lessons Learned**
By Noé Cornago
©2010 Forum of Federations, 27 pages, ISSN 1922-558X (print), CA$6

Available free online at www.forumfed.org

# McGill-Queen's University Press  /  www.mqup.ca

## Please send me the following Booklets

☐ Constitutional Origins, Structure, and Change ... (2916-0)      CA $12.95
☐ Distribution of Powers and Responsibilities ... (2974-8)      CA $12.95
☐ Legislative, Executive and Judicial Governance ... (3163-7)      CA $12.95
☐ Practice of Fiscal Federalism ... (3302-8)      CA $12.95
☐ Dialogues on Constitutional Origins ... (2939-X)      CA $12.95
☐ Dialogues on Distribution of Powers ... (2940-3)      CA $12.95
☐ Dialogues on Legislative, Executive, and Judicial ... (2941-1)      CA $12.95
☐ Dialogues on Fiscal Federalism ... (3196-3)      CA $12.95
☐ Dialogues on Foreign Relations ... (3271-7)      CA $12.95
☐ Dialogues on Local Government ... (3319-2)      CA $12.95

Total: _____

## Postage

North America: $5.00 CAD first book, $1.50 each additional.
Overseas: $5.50 CAD first book, $2.00 each additional)

Subtotal:_____
California/N.Y. State residents please add 8.25% sales tax:_____
Canadian residents please add 13% GST:_____
(GST number R132094343)
Total: _____

## Send orders to

**Direct Sales Manager, McGill-Queen's University Press**
**3430 McTavish Street, Montreal, QC H3A 1X9 Canada**

☐ Payment or credit card information must accompany order.
  Cheque/money order (Made payable to McGill-Queen's University Press).
☐ VISA      ☐ MasterCard

Credit Card number:_____

Expiry: _____/ _____/ _____

Signature: _____

Telephone/email: _____

Ship books to:_____

Name:_____

Street:_____

City:_____

Prov./State:_____      Postal/Zip code:_____